TABLE OF CONTENTS

ABOUT THE AUTHOR

I was a bit of an awkward kid. I did things like go to school in bright orange jogging pants. And I had a bowl haircut up until middle school. So it came as no surprise to my mother, when I started writing software in the 5th grade using a book I ordered through the mail called BASIC. It was a deceiving name for something resembling an unabridged dictionary. This may not seem terribly unusual today, but keep in mind however that this was in 1989, 4 years before the first commercial web browser came out. This led to the development of an order form which served as the foundation for Host1, my first significant business venture.

I grew in a suburb of New York City. On Saturdays and Sundays I would be up early out in front of the house, selling just about anything I could find in our basement — things like old books, Legos and Matchbox cars. Our house was at an intersection — it was a prime sales location — high traffic, or what certainly seemed like it at the time. Sometimes I would post flyers around the neighborhood, others times I would just count on people passing by. My mother later told me that because she couldn't stop me, she sat inside by the window the whole time I was out there to make sure no one tried to steal me.

One of my favorite books growing up was The Way Things Work. I used to have my mother read it to me as often as she could stand, as I did with all of my favorite books until I was able to read through it on my own. When I got tired of that book, I started to save up my allowance, and bought computer magazines every time I could get her to take me to the local stationary supply store.

One summer day I was out on the patio in front our house pitching a business proposal I had written to my father, asking him to lend me money to buy Apple's WebStar server software so that I could get my business up and running. My mother said I should be spending my time preparing for the next year of school. He went for it, and Host1, a business that would be a part of my life for many years, was born.

I didn't always do things the easy way. Later on when my competitors to Host1 started offering 24 hour a day support, I decided I would do the same. I set my Blackberry wireless email device to ring at the maximum volume every time an email was sent to my company's support address. I volunteered as an Emergency Medical Technician in high school, and my pager would sometimes go off 2 or 3 times on a school night, so I thought I could handle it. The whole 24 hour support thing lasted about 3 months until I found a company in India who I contracted with to handle support requests while I was sleeping.

Each time I hit a road block I bought a book and read it. Looking at the bookshelves in my apartment, I probably went through about a thousand books on business, technology & law. I spent hundreds of hours choosing the right books at Barnes & Noble and thousands of hours reading them. Although in each instance, I eventually found all of the information that I needed, it became painfully clear that there was no comprehensive reference book available written by a practitioner—I have a rule that I will only buy books written by people who have done what they are talking about because I want to work with a clear picture of the way things are. I probably would have insisted on doing things the hard way anyway, but you don't have to.

In addition to Host1 and my own reading, my perspective and knowledge are informed by work experiences at companies including the New York Stock Exchange, Merck, Volvo Corporate, Toys R' Us Corporate, Bear Stearns, Deutsche Bank, creating software used to trade billions of dollars at a finance startup, and starting a charitable foundation, all by the age of 25. If a guide like this had been available while I was building my business, I would have saved a lot of time, energy and money. I hope that you will find this to be a practical and comprehensive resource.

DISCLAIMER

The legal, accounting and tax advice contained in this book is the opinion of the author.

Legal, accounting and tax advice should always be sought from a certified professional.

COPYRIGHT NOTICE

Accounting Statements

&

Financial Projections

"I have always been amazed how many smart businessmen keep their books in such a way that they can't tell how much money they are making or losing"

John D. Rockefeller, Sr.

Accounting statements should accurately represent your company's true financial condition so that you know what financial resources you have available. To do this, it helps to keep your statements in a way that is easily understood. If you present them to outside parties, they can be reorganized by a professional to meet accounting standards.

General Ledger. The general ledger is simply a document where you add a line for each transaction that includes the date, amount, category and sender or recipient. Transactions in the general ledger are later aggregated by category when compiling other financial statements.

General Ledger

Category	Date	In/Out	To/From
Phone & Internet	4/24	128.67	AT&T
Rent	4/25	2000.00	Jones Inc.
Sales	4/27	500.00	Chris Smith

Income Statement. An income statement shows all money coming in and going out by category.

Income Statement

	2008	2009	2010
Sales	100,000	250,000	500,000
Expenses			
Rent	25,000	25,000	25,000
Utilities	2,500	2,500	2,500
Maintenance	3,000	3,000	3,000
Ads/Promotion	25,000	50,000	75,000
Legal	5,000	2,500	2,500
Accounting	1,500	1,500	1,500
Insurance	6,000	6,000	6,000
Phone & Internet	5,000	6,000	7,000
Website	5,000	1,500	1,500
Office Supplies	1,500	1,000	1,000
Salary & Benefits	150,000	250,000	400,000
	229,500	322,300	472,800
	-129,500	-72,300	27,000
Interest Paid	3,000	2,500	2,000
Depreciation	8,000	5,000	3,000
Pre-Tax Income	-140,500	-73,000	22,000
Taxes	0	0	7,126
	-140,500	-73,000	14,874

Balance Sheet. A balance sheet shows the current book value of a company, including total debt and available cash.

Balance Sheet

Assets

Cash	100,000	100,000	100,000
Inventory	0	0	0
Property	0	0	0
Equipment	25,000	30,000	40,000
Total Assets	125,000	130,000	140,000
Accounts Receivable	5,000	10,000	8,000
Total Depreciation	25,000	35,000	40,000
	105,000	100,000	193,000

Liabilities

Debt	50,000	150,000	150,000
Accounts Payable	0	65,000	98,000
	50,000	215,000	248,000

Equity

Cash Investments	500,000	250,000	250,000
Retained Profits	-50,000	50,000	250,000
	450,000	300,000	500,000

Cashflows. A statement of cashflows shows the cash a business has available at the beginning and end of each period.

Statement of Cash Flows

	2008	2009	2010
Starting Cash	250,000	180,000	170,000

Income	0	10,000	90,000
Expenses	70,000	90,000	110,000
Ending Cash	180,000	100,000	150,000

Financial Projections

Financial projections usually take the form of a 3 to 5 year income statement, balance sheet and statement of cash flows, where, instead of listing the current and past years as the column headers future years are listed.

When calculating operational expenses, remember that they are either fixed or variable, and that variable expenses are usually tied to sales volume. When making projections, there is often a tendency to overestimate sales and underestimate costs. Information on projecting income can be found in the chapter on Marketing.

Certified Financial Statements

Accounting statements presented to outside parties such as creditors and investors should be prepared and signed by a Certified Public Accountant for independent validation and partial liability coverage. If you have a Board of Directors, The Audit Committee is charged with overseeing this process.

Software

When financials are done with spreadsheet software, as opposed to by hand or in a word processor, values can be dynamically re-calculated so that changes to any single number are reflected across the entire accounting statement.

Banking and accounting software that synchronizes electronically with your various checking, savings, investment and credit accounts can provide you with an integrated real-time view of total cash and credit available. While nearly all bank accounts can be accessed through a bank's website, with multiple accounts, keeping track of balances, transactions, and payments is often cumbersome and time consuming. You may want to use desktop software that can consolidate all of your account balances, payments, and transactions.

If you don't have existing financial software, ask which software your bank supports. If you have existing accounting software, and do not already have a bank, be sure to choose one that has the ability to allow you to synchronize your account data with your existing accounting systems.

Cash Management

The ultimate cause of almost all business failures is a lack of cash. Customers' leave, loan payments come due – it all ends with a lack of cash. Cash management needs to be at the forefront of your mind every day from day one. This may seem obvious, but it's surprising how many people lose this focus and their money. Here's a basic rule: only spend money when you have it and when not doing so prevents the growth of your business.

Choosing a Bank

If you choose a bank that has the interest and ability to work with a business your size and in your industry, they may be more likely to have employees who will be able to help you succeed.

Visit the local branch of a couple of banks to determine the quality of the people you would be working with – ask what types of accounts and services they have available. Employee quality determines the success of any organization, and in turn, the success of your relationship with them.

If the account representative at the bank wants to explain all of the financial products and services they have available, take the time to listen, ask questions and learn. Keep in mind however, that bank employees receive different bonuses for different products sold, so what they're recommending may not be in your best interests.

Checking Accounts

In addition to the requirements to open a personal checking account, which usually including presenting government issued photo identification as well as a signed identification card of some sort, you will need your organization's certified formation papers and taxpayer identification number (see chapter on Formation).

Cash Reserve Account

It may be a good idea to keep a supply of cash in a reserve account should you ever run into problems. You know that if you have to tap this money, you have problems, but that your organization is still alive. To do this, determine the amount of money you would need to maintain operations for six or so months, and keep this in a separate savings account or into stable investments that could be immediately sold. In addition to standard operating expenses, be sure to include cash for upcoming payments on all outstanding debts, including additional payments that must be made if interest rates are raised, and money for upcoming taxes.

Entrepreneurs

Business expenses are usually large and sporadic, while personal expenses are usually small and continuous, and large charges from vendors can be deducted from your bank account at unexpected times, so it may make sense to keep business and personal expenses separate.

Board of Directors

"Can you imagine directors who had been personally defrauded taking such a 'boys will be boys' attitude."

Warren Buffett, Chairman & CEO, Berkshire Hathaway

Purpose

The board of directors is responsible for ensuring that management properly looks after the interests of investors, employees, customers, and the community.

Non-Independent Directors

A non-independent director is someone who has a current or recent direct or indirect financial relationship with the company. Each non-independent director should be required to maintain a significant personal financial investment in the company, to provide incentive to put in the time and energy to properly oversee management.

Independent Directors

An independent director is someone who has no current or recent direct or indirect financial relationship with the company. The benefit of having a few independent directors is that because they do not have a personal financial interest in the company, they have no financial incentive to allow anything to be misrepresented. They can be particularly valuable on an audit committee where such independence will likely give investors more confidence that the financial condition of the organization is fairly represented.

For a public company to claim a director as independent, that director must meet the independent director qualification criteria of the exchange where the stock is traded.

Committees

Management & Compensation. A committee organized to review and compensate the executive officers of the firm. This committee is also responsible for overseeing processes for recruiting, retention, development, and succession of management.

Nominating & Governance. A committee organized to nominate members to the board of directors and setup the rules that govern the board of directors.

Audit. A committee organized to ensure that financial statements are complete, accurate, and fairly represent the financial condition of the company. In order for an audit committee to meet the requirements for independence, it generally must have only independent directors who are able to understand financial statements, as well as its own charter stating membership rules and responsibilities.

Insurance

Directors & Officers insurance is intended to protect the personal assets of board members. It is possible for board members who fulfill their responsibilities to still be exposed to some liability for the actions of management, and even when they are not, they may still be exposed to investor lawsuits. Companies have the option but not the obligation to pay the legal defense of its directors. Often an insurance policy will be responsible for the costs of legally defending a director up until the point he or she has been found guilty of fraud, at which point the policy may seek reimbursement for costs incurred.

Entrepreneurs

Often a person who has made a significant financial investment in a company will want to look after their investment as a member of the board of directors. However, it is important an entrepreneur to retain voting control in order to execute his or her vision.

Business Plan

&

Financing

Most venture capital firms will explain exactly what they're looking for in a business plan somewhere on their website, however a business plan typically contains the following sections: an executive summary (brief sales pitch), the company background (see chapter on Branding), product/service description and competitors (see chapter on Development), financial statements and projections (see chapter on Accounting Statements & Financial Projections), and executive biographies or resumes.

The initial purpose of a preparing and distributing a business plan is to simply get meetings with potential investors – no one is going to mail you a check. People rarely if ever get financing the first time they present a business plan because the holes in it haven't been identified and corrected.

Work your plan out with anyone you can find that is an interested listener. If you can't take them some harsh criticism on it, you might not be ready for the rest that goes along with getting your business going. When your plan has been thoroughly worked through with potential customers and investors, and they approve, you can ask those individuals to come on board.

When talking with potential investors it helps to get their commitment to the project by taking their counsel and feedback, and making them feel like they have contributed in a meaningful way. If you engage them as a source of counsel, they will be more interested in meeting with you multiple times to see how the progress they've suggested is coming and be more likely to invest.

Perhaps the best way to get favorable financing terms is to get your business going with your own money, build up a customer base and show that you need investment to continue your high rate of growth.

Sources of Cash

Personal Loans & Lines of Credit. Most people overestimate sales and underestimate costs. Always ask for more than you think you need. If applying for financing based on your personal credit, you are in a much better position to apply for loans and lines of credit when you have an existing verifiable income. You will also be in a much better position to succeed if you have cash reserve built-up before you go down the rocky road of starting a company.

Small Business Administration (SBA). The SBA guarantees banks the repayment of a loan made to a borrower when it is made according to their guidelines.

To get a loan from the SBA, you usually have to be using the money to purchase tangibles such as land, buildings, and equipment. They are less inclined to give you money for things like developing a great idea or advertising, and may require collateral for the loan, which is something of value that can be easily sold.

Individual Investors. If you don't have personal contact with wealthy individuals, there are a number of angel investor groups around the world. In addition to an online search, these investor groups can be found though start-up targeted magazines and people who provide professional services to small and medium sized businesses such as accountants, lawyers, venture capitalists, and a local bank's small business loan officer.

Venture Capitalists. Venture Capitalists can provide cash, expertise and a contact network. However the idea that Venture Capital is necessary or best for a startup, is sometimes promoted by the Venture Capital firms themselves, and may not always be true. Some firms may want too great a percent of the company or voting rights that give them the ability to replace you or may inhibit your ability to execute your vision. If you do choose to pursue venture capital, closing a deal and doing so on reasonable terms may require competing bids from multiple firms (see chapter on Strategy & Negotiation). Most venture capitalists want to cash out on their investment in 3-5 years, either through a public offering of the company's stock or a sale to a private investor group, so there may be pressure to move on that timeline. Also, each time you take new investor money, previous shareholders' ownership is reduced, which should be kept in mind when initially issuing shares to earlier investors and employees.

Bond Issuance & Private Stock Placement. Contact the corporate division of an investment banking firm. Generally you have to be seeking to raise 5 million dollars of more. If you don't have personal contacts, you can look at the Securities & Exchange Commission filings of companies that have recently issued bonds which will list the people and companies that were involved in fundraising.

Be cautious when raising money in the capital markets, as a number of games can be played at your expense. Investors may offer you financing where if your stock price drops below a certain price, they take a significant percent of your company, potentially taking ownership of your company for only the price of the initial loan, and may even use the inside information obtained while providing the loan to damage the company's stock in order to activate triggers agreed to in a loan. Investors can short sell your company's stock or take out insurance on your company's debt, and then begin a campaign against your company through the media, analysts, creditors and rating agencies in order to profit from a decline in your company's stock price or creditworthiness.

Public Stock Offering. Stock offerings usually involve a significant base fee as well as a percent of money raised and subject a company to significant additional and periodic regulatory filing requirements.

Code of Conduct

A code of conduct and ethics identifies the rules employees are required to follow in making decisions. However, this is just a start, because bad people are going to do bad things regardless of the safeguards in place so ensuring proper conduct goes back to hiring. That doesn't mean you shouldn't have a code of conduct because good people can use guidance too.

Start by writing something that will and can be followed. If the rules set out by management don't have to be followed, then why would employees follow the other decisions of management.

The simpler the message, the easier to use all of the time, but the harder to use in difficult situations, so there has to be a balance.

Sample Code of Conduct

Every employee and contractor must adhere to the following code of ethical and legal conduct.

Law

All actions must comply with relevant laws. Employees are not required to know all the governing laws, but must know them well enough to know when to seek guidance.

Resources

Every employee must make the most efficient use possible of the company's resources, as this is critical to our profitability and survival in a competitive market. Company equipment may not be used for non-company business, except for incidental personal use.

Confidentiality

No employee may use confidential information for any purpose other than conducting the business of the company. Confidential information is all non-public information that might be of use to competitors or harmful to the company and or its customers if disclosed. Examples include trade secrets; business, marketing, and service plans; engineering and manufacturing ideas and designs; databases; records including salary information and unpublished financial data.

Gifts

The purpose of entertainment and gifts in a business setting is to create good will and sound working relationships. Gifts may not be given or accepted by an employee or family member unless they are:
   1) in compliance with applicable laws or regulations,
   2) customary,
   3) not able to be construed as a bribe or pay-off and
   4) not excessive in value.

Conflicts of Interest

A conflict of interest is any relationship or benefit that may make it difficult to perform work for the company objectively. Examples include personal benefits received as a result of employment with the company while working simultaneously for a competitor, customer or supplier. All conflicts of interest must be disclosed to the board of directors.

Disclosure

All public communications made on behalf of the company are to be accurate, fair, timely and understandable.

Accounting

It is the responsibility of each employee to bring to the attention of senior management deficiencies in accounting controls he or she may become aware of that may significantly affect financial results.

Procedure

Ask first, act later. To determine whether or not you believe an ethical violation has occurred:
1) clarify the problem by making sure you have all the facts and
2) discuss the situation with your supervisor and co-workers.

If you still believe a violation of this policy may occur or may have occurred, you must report the potential violation as outlined in the next section, Reporting.

Reporting

Suspected violations of this policy must be reported to the board of directors. No retaliatory action of any kind will be permitted against anyone making such a report to the board of directors in good faith.

Reputation

If you wouldn't want it on the front page of the local paper to be read by your friends and family don't do it.

Penalties

Violations of this policy may be subject to written warning up to dismissal without pay. Violations of this policy may also subject the individual to civil liability.

Communication

Listening

If you take a genuine interest in listening to someone you will have little competition for their time. You're cheaper than a shrink and almost everyone's favorite topic of conversation is themselves. People often respond best to listening that is done with compassion and without judgment.

Becoming a better listener is an exercise in not talking about yourself. You already know everything you have to say, and are not learning anything when you're talking. Help people talk about themselves. Don't turn it back on yourself. People tend to keep relating experiences back to themselves "I know, I mean like the other day I was" so that they can talk about themselves. While showing that you share a common experience can be important, it's not important to do it every time the other person starts talking.

While someone is talking, constantly look for and commit to memory key points that you can take from what they're saying. Follow-up with questions that show you're interested and paying attention. If the conversation stalls, ask them a question about another key point.

Practice listening with people you don't know well. The more they open up to you the better job your doing of listening.

Talking

Breaking your sentences up into individual thoughts with pauses, and delivering them with varying intonation, often allows someone to better process pieces of information.

There is some value to letting someone talk uninterrupted until they're finished. If you're trying to get information from someone, and you let them talk until their thought is completely exhausted, they will often eventually say everything that is on their mind.

There are some people who insist on talking first, loudest, longest or exclusively as a power technique. There are two ways to deal with someone who, for whatever reason, consistently talks over you. The first is to keep in your mind a short list of key points that will remind you of what to say, and when the timing is appropriate, express the thoughts associated with those points. The second is to explicitly state that you'd like to say something by saying something like "just hear me out" or "let me finish".

Writing

If you keep it to a page, it is most likely to be read, and least likely to be lost. The more engaging a memo the more impact it will have. Warren Buffett in his annual report to shareholders, possibly the most widely read annual report in business, uses folksy humor and simple one line sentences to make important points.

Handwritten notes can be particularly meaningful to employees, customers or investors and they may keep them for years. Jack Welch after performance reviews would write out a note on a small piece of paper, fax over the note, and then mail the original over to arrive a few days later. Employees report having kept them more than a decade later.

Body Language

Body language can display the entire range of human emotions, often better and more freely than words. Additionally, it is much harder to lie with body language than it is with words, and for that reason, learning to quickly and accurately read body language can be invaluable. Also, your body language may accurately represent or be consistent with your thinking, and learning to identify signals will help allow you to decide which to send.

Signs of Discomfort & Aggression

Indications of discomfort include swallowing, touching some part of the face, scratching, shaking, putting up a physical barrier such as an arm, and accelerated breathing from the release of stress chemicals into the bloodstream. People often say they just had an itch, but the fact remains that if the thing that made them uncomfortable were to be taken away, there would not have been an itch. Signs of aggression include cracking of knuckles or neck, and clenched fists. These indicators may tell you when to back off or press forward on a particular topic.

Handshakes

A handshake is not an exercise in squeezing. There should be no open space between your palm and the palm of the person whose hand you're shaking. The web between your thumb and pointer finger should connect with the same spot on the recipient's hand. Keep your fingers slightly parted and firm. With your grip, sense and match their pressure up until an appropriate threshold. Practice shaking you own hand, and using different levels of pressure.

Eye Contact

A number of studies have indicated that natural eye contact is made between 40 and 60 percent of the time during conversation. When you access different parts of the brain your eyes naturally go in different directions. Learn to sense the method of eye contact the person that you're talking with uses and how to respond to make them comfortable.

Hostility & Aggression

There are several techniques to attempt to intimidate or control through physical hostility and aggression. I have found a high-correlation between these techniques and those listed in the Lies section of the Leadership & Decision Making chapter. Simulating activities that occur naturally during a fight is hostile and aggressive, and can including staring without blinking, being physically controlling by squeezing and holding during a handshake, and coming face to face within striking distance. If you encounter someone using these techniques, you may think you've angered that person, and may want to do something to placate them, but don't as this is not the case, these are simply power techniques. You can tell someone who is staring without blinking that it's hostile and aggressive and you would prefer natural eye contact, someone who is squeezing and holding your hand that it's inappropriate, and someone who tries to put their body into you can be blocked with you hand in a non-aggressive way.

Hand Gestures & Facial Expressions

Hand gestures and facial expressions, when they correspond to the words being spoken, can activate the visual part of the brain and enhance impact. To develop your ability to effectively use hand gestures or facial expressions, practice speaking very slowly in the mirror while choosing a gesture or expression for each word or thought segment as you speak.

Storytelling

Great story tellers are able to create visual imagery while at the same time keeping a story flowing, engaging and compelling. To create visual imagery, give a few details about things that could be observed with the eyes. This helps engage the visual part of the brain rather than just the auditory, and can help the story have more impact.

To keep a consistent flow, speak slowly enough that you have the next line of the story in your head. Practice writing out stories, and telling them out loud with friends.

Videotaping

Many people would be surprised to see their own body language on video. Your read of your body language on video may be significantly different from what you think you're portraying. If you take the time to record a video of yourself in a conversation with a friend, presentation or sales pitch, you will likely find that you exhibit signals that are inconsistent with your thinking. A video recording of your body language will allow you to identify and hopefully correct incongruities.

Circumstance

When reading body language, it is important to realize that it is often being presented through a person's present emotional condition and state of mind. Be careful not to firmly ascribe attributes based on a single encounter. It is difficult to know with certainty what temporary external factors might be contributing to a person's present condition.

Phone Calls

At the beginning of any phone call with a customer service representative ask for their first name and representative ID number or location and make a note of it. Use it during the conversation to make it known that you wrote it down. If you ask for it later in the call after you have a problem it seems like a threat. If you ask for it in the beginning, it makes the representative accountable. Use their name whenever you have a request they would prefer not to handle or they are thinking of transferring your call. "I would appreciate that Chris." If they know you have the ability to call back their supervisor, they may be more inclined to solve a problem and less inclined to transfer you or put you on hold indefinitely. It can also be useful if you need to follow-up to keep notes from the call in a journal.

Branding

Consistency

A consistent look and feel across an organization's public communications can help present the image an organization has itself in order.

Sitcoms have many different writers, particularly if a show spans multiple seasons, yet there is always an effort to maintain a seamlessly consistent style and voice. If all of your corporate communications were read through, would they display a consistent style and voice?

If you're not sure of what style to adopt, adopt the style of communications written by the CEO. If those are particularly bad, you can work off the best communications by a senior executive that you have available.

Layout & Design

If all corporate communications were lined up side by side would they display uniformity in layout and design? In order to make this happen, share design templates, logos, and frequently used graphics across the organization.

Story

A good story does something to capture a person's heart or imagination. Why did you start your business? How are you're different? Google started out of a dorm room at Stanford in an effort to make the world's information universally useful and accessible.

Personal and company background stories can be an important component of a customer's purchasing decision, particularly when selling services. People find a sense of comfort in knowing that the product or service that's being provided comes from someone who they can connect with and has the background to deliver as promised.

Research

Collect the background stories of companies and executives you admire or think your customers would like to buy from. Note the topics, structure and flow. These tend to includes four or five paragraphs and move from current duties, to previous employment, awards or recognitions, education, and then to location and family.

You may want to include a photo of yourself at the top of your personal background story. Having the founder or CEO of the company sign the bottom of the company story can give it more personal impact.

Portrait Photos

"Man without smiling face should not open shop"

Old Chinese Proverb

Portrait photos can convey both your personality and the personality of your organization which can influence customers purchasing decisions.

Begin by collecting an assortment of portrait photos you think your target customer would like. From the portraits, take note of hairstyle, lighting, colors, and expression. Many CEO's appear with a disarming "soccer dad" smile that portrays both confidence and strength. Hairstyles don't seem to vary much by country and culture—they are almost always short and clean. Lighting isn't artistic, but serves only to provide a very clear picture. Colors are where the personality of the executive seems to come through—bold, serious, vibrant, conservative, etc.

Many photographers use artistic lighting or are used to working with fashion models or kids. Find a photographer whose portfolio includes photos that look like the ones you want to have taken.

Logo

A good logo either has some meaning behind it, or is interesting enough to make people speculate that there's some meaning behind it – like a popular but poorly written song or book. As much as first impressions count, a logo is important, not only at the company level but for new products and services.

Research

Gather a collection of your favorite logos. Theses can be clipped from magazines, newspapers or logo design books. Picasso's biographer once wrote that his mastery came from his ability to study and take pieces of others art and assemble them into his own harmonious creation.

Digitize

Using ideas from your collection of logos, sketch your logo on paper over and over until it is exactly what you want. Once your final sketch is done, you can go to your computers image editing program. Unless you've already purchased expensive image editing or illustration software, probably the best way to get started on your logo is to use whatever paint program came with your computer. If you logo isn't done on paper, don't start work on the computer. It will provide a sense of false progress, and most likely lead to wasted time. If you don't have the graphic design skills to complete your logo on your own, going through the first steps before engaging a professional designer will allow you to better communicate what you're looking for.

Phone Numbers

Custom phone numbers have two benefits. First, customers or prospective customers may be more likely to call if they can remember your phone number. Second, it can create the impression that you put some thought into setting up your business.

Selection

Numbers and letters on a phone correspond as follows: ABC:2, DEF:3, GHI:4, JKL:5, MNO:6, PQRS:7, TUV:8, WXYZ:9. You can start by taking the letters in your organization's name, or part of its name, and identifying the corresponding numbers. For example, a business by the name of Maher Books has two options, Maher as 62437 or Books as 26657, either of which could then be used when searching for a 7 digit phone number that contains that sequence of digits, such as 212-40-BOOKS (212-406-2437) or 800-40-BOOKS (800-402-6657).

Retention

You can search for available phone numbers that contain specific digits in sequence with the phone company either by calling and asking them to search or by searching available phone numbers in the business section of their website.

Toll Free Numbers

A toll-free number bills the person called rather than the caller. It forwards a phone call to any phone number that you specify. That means that the cost of receiving calls on a toll-free number is usually the same or less as making a call to the number that called you. Toll free numbers in the United States begin with 800, 888, 877, or 866.

Signature

To help develop yours, you can take a look at signatures from various executives online. Then get a cursive handwriting development book from the local book store and do the practice exercises in it. It will probably be in the kids section. Practice each letter of your signature individually. When your have your signature finalized, scan it into your computer or have someone scan it for you, so that you can add it to computerized documents.

Entrepreneurs

Focus on bringing in money. Don't let work on ideas presented in this section hold you up, as you can get by with just having a business name in the beginning.

Contracts

Doing business without a contract is like driving without a seatbelt: it's not a problem unless there's a problem.

Writing

A contract should cover the situations that may occur during the course of business and how each will be handled. A generic sample contract is appended to this chapter. You can look at your competitors' contracts on the internet for ideas as to what situations should be covered.

It is important to first write your own contracts, rather than have a lawyer do it, if only as an exercise so that you can think about exactly how your client relationships will work. After it is written, seek the review of a legal professional to ensure that you have included all necessary protections for yourself and that what you have written is legally enforceable. Lawyers would have you think it's too difficult to write your own contracts, but no one knows your business better than you.

It may be best to use a lawyer with experience in your industry so that they are not learning your industry while they're charging you. Be sure to tell your lawyer you want to maintain the contracts use of everyday language as it is exceptionally rare that there is anything at all more legally binding about using legal jargon.

It is particularly important to remember when it comes to selling that an everyday-language one-page contract is most likely to be signed. A prospective client is likely to feel comfortable signing a one page document without consulting a lawyer. Take it over a page, and they start to wonder what's in it — you might as well make it 20 pages.

If you do take your contract over one page, and you want your client to actually read it, it is a good idea to require each section of the contract be initialed.

Reviewing

You'll usually find that most people you communicate with at your partner organization have no idea what's in their contract. Whenever evaluating new partners, take the time to understand how the relationship will work, as outlined in their contract—at least one of you should know what it says. It will also give you a chance to ask questions you might not have thought of.

Review each line of the contract and on a photocopy underline the conditions that could be problematic while staying on the look out for any deal-breakers. If you choose to do business with this partner, keep your notes accessible, particularly on potentially problematic policies. If a term in the contract simply isn't acceptable, find out who has the authority to change it, and try to get them to do so by emphasizing the value of the relationship and your desire to be fair and reasonable. If it is a contract with a large and powerful company, and you're not one, they may not be willing to make any exceptions to their standard contract. At that point, it's a judgment call based on the level of risk you'd be taking on.

Precautions

A person can not be legally obligated to perform an illegal activity. A contract could be made to perform an illegal activity, but that wouldn't that make the contract legally binding. For that reason, not all contract clauses are legal, even if the contract has been signed by both parties. The legality of a contract is not tested until it reaches a court. The general rule is that a contract and all of its parts must be "reasonable" to a "reasonable person".

A contract or a change to a contract will only be considered valid in court if it was made by someone who is formally authorized to make contracts for the company. You could walk into Starbucks and ask a barista to sign off on selling the company, but Starbucks wouldn't be obligated to make the sale. The President, CEO and Chairman all have authority to bind the company to a contract and from there it varies, as specified in the company's by-laws and state law. Some contracts even require the approval of a company's Board of Directors.

If your contract is with a big company and someone tells you they have authority to sign contracts, they probably mean they have authority from their boss. Ask if the authority for someone with their title is stated in their company's by-laws – maybe even ask for a signed or certified copy of their by-laws for your records. If they're not authorized to sign a contract it could be invalidated in court.

Beware of contracts that are complicated and ambiguous. A contract may complicated and ambiguous for one of two reasons: either it was written entirely by a lawyer, or it was written that way so that claims can be made later on that aren't really there. The second reason is really something to watch out for. If you can't understand the contract, it may be because you're not supposed to.

A faxed signature is generally not legally binding in court, because of how easily it could be forged, and so anything other than a signature in ink may be symbolic.

For contracts involving large sums of time or money, it is often a good idea to sign the contract in the presence of an independent witness. When choosing a witness, ask yourself, "Would this person convince a jury?" One option is a notary public with whom you have no significant financial relationship.

Sample Agreement

Applicable Law. This Agreement shall be governed in all respects by the laws of the city and state of New York.

Exclusivity. This Agreement constitutes the entire understanding between Company and Client.

Initiation. The initiation of this Agreement is the date that this Agreement is received by Company after having been signed by both Client and Company. The service term begins on Initiation.

Payment. Payment in full must clear for service to start but does not affect Initiation or Agreement's binging nature.

Services. Company is a provider of search engine positioning services. Company will list the webpage located at the address specified at the end of this agreement on the 1st page of Google's search results for the search term specified at the end of this agreement for the amount specified at the end of this agreement for the period of one year. If during one year from the Initiation date, Client's website falls from the top of Google, Company will work to move the site back to the top. Company may at its discretion work to increase Client's visibility for additional search terms and in search engines other than Google. Service will renew in subsequent years.

Confidentiality. Neither Company nor Client may share personal information obtained during the course of business with any third party, unless doing so becomes reasonably necessary under the provisions of this Agreement.

Subcontractors. Company, at its discretion and in order to provide the best price to Client, may use subcontractors.

Liability. Company is not responsible for losses to Client's business as a result of performance of services under this agreement, not limited to but including potential losses from: (1) visibility in the search results at a time that is not ideal, (2) links to or from sites considered to be objectionable, (3) not increasing visibility in the search results and (4) dropping from the search results.

Disputes. Either Client or Company may elect to settle a dispute though binding arbitration in the borough of Manhattan in the city and state of New York. Costs related to the proceeding will be allocated by the arbitrator(s).

Marketing. Company may use Client's name, company, website, search term and comments in promotional material.

Pricing. Company may choose to increase or decrease its yearly service fee in subsequent years.

Responsibilities. Client's responsibilities include: (1) creating a brief title and description meta-tag for the agreed upon web page that each prominently include the agreed upon search phrase (2) maintaining a link from the agreed upon webpage to a new webpage on their site that will list other websites—this list will be generated with data from Company, by inserting a segment of code, written in a standard computer language, into this new web page.

Termination. If Client does not carry out their responsibilities under this Agreement, Company may choose to terminate service to Client without refund or liability. Client may at any time and for any reason choose to terminate the services of Company without refund or liability. Company may terminate Agreement after the initial service period.

Refunds. A full refund will be made to Client if Company is not able to list their webpage for specified search term within 6 months of Initiation.

Company   **Client**

Company_____
Name_____   Name_____
Title_____   Title_____
Date_____   Date_____
Signature_____   Signature_____

Courts

Arbitration

&

Mediation

"Never stir up litigation. A worse man can scarcely be found than one who does this."

Abraham Lincoln

There are a number of dispute resolution methods that vary in time and cost. Please be sure to read the chapters on Leadership & Decision Making and Strategy & Negotiation before pursuing these options.

Preparing a Dispute

If you are considering initiating a formal dispute resolution process, the first step is to prepare a brief list of claims. The claims should be ordered by date, and broken up into individual claims that the other party will be sure to either dispute or not dispute. The task then, is to provide supporting documentation for the claims that the other party will dispute. It is also helpful to prepare a list of claims that the other party would make, whether or not the claims are true. When this is done, bring it to the other party and see if they will agree to some sort of settlement.

Mediation

Mediation is simply a discussion facilitated by an independent third party. A mediator has no legal authority, so there can be no legally enforceable outcome to the discussions with a mediator. Mediation of a dispute is one of the least expensive and least damaging ways to handle a problem. A mediator has to use influence rather than authority to help you both achieve a reasonable settlement.

Arbitration

Arbitration is a formal legal proceeding run by a person who is certified by the American Arbitration Association to handle your proceeding. Arbitrators are often retired judges with experience in your industry. As a rule, you give up your right to a trial with a jury when you agree ahead of time to resolve any disputes through arbitration.

Courts

Courts are the most expensive way to resolve a dispute and going to court is often a misallocation of resources. Court disputes often take months to resolve if not years. While you may in the end receive a positive verdict, there is usually some delay in receiving money awarded and lawyers' fees will often take up much of the award. In the end, if you took the resources (time, energy, money) that would go into a court dispute, and used them to move other things forward, you may in the end be much better off.

Lawyers can be paid on retainer, by the hour, or on a contingency fee basis. Lawyers working on retainer will generally provide you up to a fixed number of hours of their time per month for a monthly fee. Lawyers working on a contingency fee basis will be paid only when they win money for you, but for them to invest their own time and money in a case, they have to be pretty certain that they can win significant compensation.

Credit Rating

A credit rating is intended to assess the probability that an individual or organization will pay back borrowed money. Believing that past behavior is the best predictor of future behavior, credit rating agencies primarily use your payment history in determining your credit rating. There is no quick or easy way to boost your credit rating, but it can be legitimately done. The first step is getting your credit report from one of the sources listed below.

Private Companies

Dunn & Bradstreet (http://www.dnb.com) maintains a credit profile on all government-registered businesses, and regularly request copies of all businesses newly registered with each state government. A file will usually be available on your business several months after your incorporation or partnership papers are filed. If you are in a hurry or do not see your business listed after a few months, be prepared with your incorporation documents and EIN (see the chapter on Formation), and give them a call.

Public Companies

For publicly traded companies, credit records are associated with either a CUSIP or ISI number. Ratings are provided by Standard & Poors, Moodys, and Fitch, though some companies are not considered large enough to receive rating coverage. You can contact each rating agency individually to request initiation of rating coverage. A rating will be used when selling debt to investors in the public markets.

Personal

A business owner has the option of applying for business loans based on his or her personal credit history. This may be done if the business has either a brief or poor credit history. The first step is getting a copy of your credit report which can be done online or on the phone from one of the three primary personal credit reporting agencies: TransUnion, Experian and Equifax. You will be required to provide your name, social security number and date of birth. Once you have obtained a copy from each agency, review the reports looking for negative items and/or irregularities.

Removing Negative Information

Negative items on a credit report can lead to a lower loan amount and higher interest rate. In order to request changes to your report, you will need a report number which can only be obtained from reports issued directly by the individual agencies.

It is often thought that the best way to remove a negative item from a credit report is to dispute the item with the credit reporting agency—this should be a last resort. The best way to permanently remove a negative item from your report is to have it removed from the computers of the company who has you on record as owing them money so that it is not resubmitted to the agency at a later date. Once you have paid off the debt, submit a request with the credit agencies to contact the company to verify that the debt has been paid.

When deciding to negotiate a payment to a creditor, even if you consider it invalid, take into account how much it will cost you to keep a negative item on your report, and how much it will cost to get rid of it.

After the impact of negative items has been minimized or removed, ensure that all positive credit accounts have been recorded with each agency, and submit supporting documentation if necessary.

Tax Liens

Tax-liens can be issued by any government agency including the DMV and courts. Tax-liens will stay on your report indefinitely, but once you pay them, they are usually dropped from your report almost immediately.

Collections

If you have any items from a collection agency on your credit report, these can have a substantial negative impact. Collections can be handled and reported by an internal collections department or an outside collection service.

Some companies send bills to their internal collections department before they send them to an outside collection service. An internal collections department still has some concern for your relationship with the company and may be the easier to deal with.

The first thing an outside collection service does when they receive an account is to put it on your credit report, hoping you'll eventually notice then give them a call and agree to pay. The outside collection company has typically purchased the debts of a company. Say a company has $1 million in debts deemed uncollectible. They then sell these debts to a collection agency for $100,000. The collection agency then may hope to get people to pay a total of $300,000. Collection agency representatives are authorized to settle for less than the total debt, usually around 50%. When paying the collection agency, strongly request that they notify the company they bought the debt from so that the debt is also removed from that company's computers.

Submitting a Dispute

Disputes can be submitted online or through postal mail. You generally must attach a photocopy of a government issued ID to your dispute letter. If your documents are not properly in order the credit bureau may not fully consider your request and send you a dismissal letter

If you are willing to sign and notarize your dispute, this can add some weight to it. Once the agency has reviewed your dispute and made a ruling there isn't much else that can be reasonably done.

Personal Statements

Consumer credit agencies are required by law to allow you to include a short statement at the end of your credit report. This is only useful if your credit report is reviewed by a human who has some discretion in deciding your loan. This is often not the case because once a loan is made, although you make payments directly to the bank, it is usually sold by the bank with other loans to large investors who do not look at these statements.

Customer Service

Sales & Support Chat

Instant messaging over the Internet can be an easy and comfortable way for a prospective customer to initiate contact and an efficient way to provide some support services to existing customers. . To initiate a conversation, a website visitor clicks on a link on your website for live chat, a box pop-ups for a chat session, and if someone at your company is logged into the system, the chat session begins. This service can be setup fairly quickly with an outside service provider who can be found by searching the Internet.

Interactive Voice Response

Interactive Voice Response (IVR) systems allow a caller to interact with a computer and either route the caller to the appropriate person or provide information. When developing the call scripts for an IVR, it is best to take phone calls yourself and seeing what customers ask and need. From those conversations, develop a flowchart indicating all of the different directions that a call could go and how you would like each situation to be resolved.

Once the flow chart is done, begin recording voice prompts for the system. The easiest and least expensive way to develop voice prompts is to begin by recording each prompt in your voice. The easiest way to get a persons voice into the system is to call the system and leave messages. Most systems can be managed through a web browser, where these messages can be downloaded and the uploaded as voice prompts.

Once the voice prompts have been finalized, you may want to find the employee with the best phone voice, rent a studio for a couple of hours, and have all the prompts re-recorded. Recording time can be rented at almost any recording studio for a reasonable per hour fee. The sound files will need to be saved individually and converted to the file format used by your system, which can be done by the studio recording the voice prompts.

Call Centers

Call centers can provide everything from answering services to order taking and technical support.

Selection

To find call center services start with an Internet search. Going with a company that is already used by a company in your industry may save time and increase quality as the company may already have industry specific knowledge.

Many of the companies that offer call center services are located in Asia, where educated people who speak fluent English cost less to employ. Many call centers provide training on a proper accent and dialect as well as customs.

Answering Services

You provide the scripts for the operator to read and they do the rest. They can instantaneously send messages to you or your organization by pager, voicemail, fax, email or telephone relay.

Order Taking

If you are selling a product or service by phone, either provide the ordering staff with an order form that they can fill out and fax over to you or provide them access to your organization's online ordering system to input orders on behalf of clients.

Customer Service

Customer service often requires an intimate knowledge of an organization. A customer service representative needs to be able to use their judgment to make a fully informed decision on behalf of a customer and the organization. For these reasons, customer service including billing support may be difficult to send outside of the organization.

Development

"I can't provide you with job security. Only satisfied
customers can do that."

Jack Welch
Former Chairman & CEO
General Electric

If you make a bad product, you'll be sure to have enough
for everyone who wants one.

Competitors

When beginning to build a new product, service or
organization, analyze each competitive offering and what
advantages or disadvantages each has relative to your
offering.   This can be done in a matrix like the one
below.

Payroll Software Providers

	Price	Support	Synchronization
QuickBooks	$50	No	Yes
Payroll Plus	$80	24x7	Yes
Popular Payroll	$40	No	No

This will help in deciding whether or not to pursue a particular development opportunity and what features should be included.

Customer Focus

Selling requires that you personally interact with customers. This does not mean that all of your sales have to be done one on one or that you have to interact with every single customer. It just means that in determining how to develop and market your products or services, you need the feedback that you can only get from constant customer interaction. Services need to be developed based on what the customer needs, not what you think the customer needs. They are an integral part of the development process for new service offerings. Who wouldn't use a product that they designed themselves? It's not about you, it's about them.

Three groups must collaborate in the development of a product: customers, sales and engineering. If sales were to develop the specifications for a product and hand it off to engineering, features might be unrealistic or lacking, and if engineering developed the product alone, time might be spent developing features that aren't particularly important to customers. Sales, development and customers have to work together.

Risks

A great product that is too far ahead of its time or is not attractive to your existing customer base is a financial risk. Engineers often like to work do work that is cutting edge rather than market or customer focused. Although many developers are more comfortable working in isolation, it is important that they are allowed and encouraged to interact often and directly with customers. Developing a superior product is great only if it's what people want. Don't waste your resources: give customers what they want. Development needs to understand that if they don't develop something that the company can sell, then no money comes in, and if no money comes in, you won't be able to pay them well if at all.

Prioritize

Prioritize development tasks by the order in which they affect revenues. It is much easier to take substantial profits out of high revenues than to take them out of low revenues. Building revenues and building profits can be done alternatively.

Profitability

Profits attract competitors. If you are making big profits on a particular product or service, it will likely attract others into that business and drive down your profits. If you have a product or service that's profitable, legal and ethical, put your resources into doing it over and over, selling as much as you can, because as quick as that profit center came, it can go. And be prepared with the next product or service to take its place.

Outsourcing

Software development and engineering are particularly prone to outsourcing because technical skills are not bound by culture, language or location. However, collaborating with developers in another country is a skill that requires a conscious effort to develop as there may be some difficulty in communicating with and managing employees living in a different time zone, who have a different native language and culture. Some companies send development abroad only to bring much of it back.

Entrepreneurs

Entrepreneurs often wait too long to put themselves out on a limb and see if customers will buy. Bringing in money is progress—not spending it. And while you're busy planning and building your infrastructure, your competitors may be out selling.

Distribution

Barcodes

Barcodes represent, and radio frequency tags emit, a unique number that identifies a vendor, product and price. This number is intended to help a retail store track and sell a product.

To put a barcode on a product that will be universally recognized, a company must register for a vendor identification number with the Global Standards Group. Fees vary and are determined in part by a company's annual revenue. The Global Standards Group maintains a database of all registered vendors and product codes which large retail stores then integrate into their inventory management systems. Their website can be found through a quick Internet search.

Once you are issued a vendor identification number, you can begin printing barcodes for individual products. To print the barcode, you will need a barcode font on your computer which can be found through an Internet search. The barcode font, instead of displaying numbers, will display representative bars.

RFID Tags

Radio frequency tags, referred to as RFID (Radio Frequency Identification) tags, emit radio waves that contain a product's universal identification number. Using a radio scanner, RFID tags allow large boxes in a warehouse to be identified without having to be moved. These can be purchased pre-programmed in bulk quantities.

ISBN

ISBNs are 13 digit numbers used to identify written works that can be represented by a barcode. These numbers can be purchased for a reasonable fee from ISBN International (http://www.isbn-international.org/).

Shipping

Prices can vary substantially between shipping providers as some are optimized for a particular package size and distance.

Retail

Call up or visit the store or the headquarters of the store where you would like to sell your product, ask to speak with the buyer or head of merchandising, present your product, and ask if they would be willing to carry it.

Entrepreneurs

If you only need an identification number for one or two products, there are companies that will sell you a individual numbers.

You can always ask the stores you want to sell your product in whether or not they will accept your product without a barcode before going through the process of getting one. If they will, you may want to wait to get a barcode until not having one makes selling your product significantly more difficult or you start making significant sales.

Employees

"I learned early in my career that if you want to be a
winner you have to work with winners"

Warren Buffett
Chairman & CEO
Berkshire Hathaway

Hiring

You can screw up almost anything but hiring. The
success of an organization depends on no greater factor
than its people. If you have the right people working for
you, with their help, other things tend to fall into place.
Good people attract and retain other good people, and the
converse is also true.

Recruitment

Employees can be found through personal contacts,
networking events, online networking sites, classified ads
and recruiters. You can put the word out to your contact
network that you're looking to hire, visit trade shows or
industry sponsored events, contact a few headhunters,
and search online job sites. To develop an idea of
exactly what you're looking for and what you will have
to pay, you can start by looking online at job descriptions
of positions similar to the one you want to fill. Job

descriptions typically include company background, expected responsibilities, prior experience, educational background, pay and benefits. If you post an advertisement for a job, be sure to review competing advertisements to see if there is anything you left out or could improve upon in your own advertisement.

Resumes

Past performance is often the best predictor of future performance. However, be careful not to be too impressed by any single item or group of closely dated items. Accomplishments may have been more a reflection of the environment a person was in or the support they were given and no longer have available. Accomplishments can build on each other like a snowball rolling down a hill. This can create a misperception as to the value a person would bring to your company. Conversely, some people may have never found an environment or opportunity where they could really excel. What matters is a person's ability to contribute value to your organization.

Education

Keep in mind that while education may be more important than anything in the world, and if there's a silver bullet to the world's problems it's education, that probably 99.9% of the greatest and most successful people in history didn't even go to college. A high GPA demonstrates that someone can do what they're told and do it well, which can make them a valuable employee.

Interviewing

It's worth taking a couple of hours to talk with a candidate about their past experiences. You will be spending countless hours with this person if hired so you might as well start spending some time talking now. Discuss each point on their resume thoughtfully and exhaustively.

Having more than one person interview a candidate, no matter how thorough you are, can provide valuable additional information. They may be able to establish a different rapport and pickup additional information that you didn't. Each member of the team should have the opportunity to talk with the candidate as each will likely be spending significant time with him or her if a job is offered and accepted.

The hiring manager has to factor in bias. Interviewers may have a personal preference for a candidate or a particular candidate may be threatening to their responsibilities in some way, and may have an incentive to misrepresent, even unintentionally, their conversations with the prospect.

If you don't have a resume available to you when you talk with the person, you can tell them a little bit about the company and the job you have in mind, and then ask them to talk a little bit about their relevant personal and professional experience. Also account for the fact some people are great at interviewing and others are terrible, but that you're not hiring to person to interview, you're hiring them to do a job.

If you hire someone who has personal goals that fit within the organization, the organization and the individual can grow together and support each other. In addition to goals, ask about talents, interests and passions, and work to figure out how those might be useful within the company. Listen for values and how they have used them to make decisions in the past. And probe for the exact individual contribution to each accomplishment presented.

Technical Interviewing

As someone with a programming background, I have found that the best way to identify a great programmer is to be a great programmer. However, if you don't have a strong technical background, there are two ways I have seen to get around this. One is to exhaustively discuss past technical projects the person has worked on to determine their exact role and contribution. The other is to look at work samples developed exclusively by that individual.

A technique I have seen consistently used by people with strong technical backgrounds that doesn't yield great results is to lookup and ask technical and theory based questions that aren't relevant to the job. MIT even has a course where the exclusive purpose is to prepare people to answer these types of questions. This is not a productive use of time, and you should instead focus on the prospects individual contributions to past projects and whether or not they are consistent with what you need done.

Non-Compete & Non-Disclosure Agreements

Depending on the work the employee will be doing and what level of access they have to confidential information, it may make sense to have the employee sign agreements that they will not disclose certain information obtained during the course of employment and that they may not work for a competitor for a period of time after leaving your company.

Application Forms

If you haven't developed an internal application form, standard hiring application forms can be purchased from an office supply store. It is a good idea just to have some sort of application as a place for the person to list contact information for references.

Reference Checks

A reference can be from a professional, personal, academic or community context that can potentially provide useful insight. Before making a final hiring decision, it may be a good idea to check a couple references to get a more complete picture of the applicant. It's also a good idea to check the references who clearly know the applicant the best as they would likely be most interested in talking with you and willing and able to provide the most information. Even if friends or family may not provide the most reliable information they will provide the most information.

If there is any negative information presented, allow the applicant an opportunity to respond to it (see chapter on Leadership & Decision Making). An applicant may have had a horrible former employer, and you might get a horrible review, but without asking the applicant, for all you know it could be for exactly the reasons you'd want to hire the person.

When verifying an achievement claimed on a resume, remember that the person who received credit for something is not always the person who was responsible. Also, there can be a disconnect between contribution and recognition with particularly talented people. It is important to probe for and understand the candidate's individual contributions.

Background Check

There are a number of low cost services that can be found online that will perform a standard background check of criminal records, educational degree verification, credit records, and title, salary and dates of former employers.

Humility & Arrogance

There are two types of arrogance, and it is important to distinguish between them: intellectual and personal. Personal arrogance is when someone thinks they're better than other people and lets others know that. Intellectual arrogance is when someone won't listen even when you are willing to listen, and doesn't learn from mistakes. It is possible to display personal arrogance because of a lack of intellectual arrogance, with a person knowing that the way they do things is simply better. Personal arrogance is annoying while intellectual arrogance is damaging.

Compensation

Employees can be compensated with pay, benefits, learning and responsibility.

To determine fair market compensation for a specific job, look at the advertisements on online job sites that are the most similar. Develop a chart listing along the top attributes including base salary, bonus, retirement contributions, health benefits, potential hours, and vacation time, and for each job record relevant information in a new row. Compare your offer with each of the other jobs to help determine how you are you going to develop a competitive compensation package.

A positive work environment is free to provide and often an overlooked form of compensation. If employees are happy in their jobs they're unlikely to leave for the same amount of money somewhere else.

Stock

Stock in a company can provide a powerful incentive to see a company succeed as employees have the opportunity to make a significant profit if the company does well. The drawback in issuing stock to employees is that new shares decrease the ownership stake of those who have existing shares.

Stock options

Stock options are the option to buy stock from the company at a later date at a set price. The effect is that employees get to profit from appreciation in the stocks price, but if the stock does not increase in value above the price set, the option is not worth anything.

Quarterly Profit Sharing

One way to rally employees around profitability is to allocate a percent of profits each quarter that will be distributed to employees. This can also help boost morale, reduce waste and improve productivity.

Performance Reviews

Performance reviews are intended to help an organization achieve peak performance. When done properly, they can also help people become more productive and fulfilled by their jobs.

Establish at the beginning of a review period specific criteria for what it means to deliver results. Evaluation criteria should be setup to reward the behaviors that you want. Develop clear evaluation criteria up-front in conjunction with each employee, and stick to them.

Some people don't have the ability to distinguish between criticism of themselves and criticism of their work, and will become hostile and aggressive in response to criticism. However it is still important for a performance review to be honest, straightforward, candid and comprehensive.

Types

There are generally four types of performers.

First, the best employees deliver results and live the company's values. These are the company's most valuable assets.

Second, are employees who don't deliver great results but live the company's values. They can be valuable.

Third, are employees who deliver results but don't live the company's values. These employees are difficult to get rid of because there will be short term cost, but if they are continually permitted to behave in a way that is inconsistent with the company's values it may ultimately erode the foundation of the company, and so the long term cost can be significantly greater.

Fourth, are employees who don't deliver results and don't live the company's values, and so obviously have to be fired, but before you do that read the chapter on Leadership and Decision Making.

Recency Bias

If performance reviews are only done once a year, some people will be inclined to tout accomplishments and perform at their peak near review time. This can create a false perception of their contributions. To account for this, you can maintain a journal where you regularly record the contributions of employees under your supervision.

Ranking

Ranking employees against one and other is a great system in the short term or when going through a period of transition, however, in the long-term, this method can hinder cooperation and teamwork.

Listen

You have to care about how an employee feels to the extent that the way they feel is reasonable and affects performance. Take time during the meeting to listen to everything an employee has to say without cutting them off. An employee may have specific legitimate problems with you or your management, and they should be candidly discussed without repercussion and resolved as best as is possible, so that the organization can achieve optimal performance. It's a better time to listen than during an exit interview.

Review Meeting

You may want to ask an employee about their talents, interests and goals, and if possible modify their job to accommodate those, as people usually perform best when they are interested in what they are doing. Work with the employee to develop goals for the next review period and ask the employee how you can help him deliver on these goals. An effective manager consistently works to help employees achieve these objectives.

Training & Education

Encouraging and supporting employees to continually develop new skills will allow your organization increase productivity.

From the wheel, to tractors, to personal computers, humans have always used technology to increase productivity. The objective is not to train employees to become technology workers, but to help them more thoroughly integrate technology into their daily work to continually find new ways to become more productive.

In an increasingly competitive global economy, learning has to become a lifetime commitment rather that one that only occurs early in life or only in educational institutions, or an organization and its workers will eventually lose out to global competition.

Firing

"Homer, the plant called and said if you don't come in today, don't bother coming in Monday."
"Woo-hoo. 4 day weekend."

Marge & Homer J. Simpson

Reasons

Employees can generally be fired for non-performance, because of financial constraints or misconduct.

Firing for non-performance is like pruning a tree. Each dying branch of a tree takes life-giving nutrients from the rest of the tree. If you cut the dying branch off early, those nutrients can be used by the rest of the tree. Cut your losses on bad hires quickly and properly. Firing should never be a surprise and it should always be done after more than one candid performance review. Before removing an employee for suspected misconduct, be sure to read the chapter on Leadership & Decision Making.

Legal Implications

It is helpful to maintain legitimate, non-discriminatory and documented performance reviews.

Healthcare Coverage

An employer is generally required under federal law to allow a former employee to continue healthcare coverage, and notify them of this upon employment termination, as long as the employee pays the insurance premium. More information on this can be found in the Healthcare chapter.

Formation

Location

The physical location of a business can have a significant impact on its long term success. Certain cities have existing and affordable resources in place that support particular industries.

Educational Institutions

Certain cities have educational institutions and specific industries that have co-evolved and support each others' growth. Examples include business schools at Columbia University and New York University the financial community. Stanford University and Silicon Valley technology community. University of California San Diego and the University of San Diego and biotech firms. These relationships help shape academic programs and provide students who graduate with skills in your industry.

Established Employee Base

Choosing an area with an established employee base in your industry will make recruiting easier and retention more difficult. The biggest cost is that employees can more easily move between companies for higher pay without uprooting their families and personal lives. The biggest benefit is the ability to expand rapidly with highly skilled employees.

Investor Base

With newer industries, major investors will often be located in the same areas as the businesses they fund.

Acquirers

If you are looking to sell your business at any point, your employees and facilities will need to be integrated with the buyer's employees and facilities. The less geographical distance between your business and your buyer the more practical the acquisition. If you are looking to be bought, it is most practical to be physically located near the company that would by you.

Employer Identification Number

If you are forming an organization that has employees other than yourself, you will need an Employer Identification Number (EIN) which is a number assigned by the United States Internal Revenue Service and is required for a business to open a bank account, pay taxes and have a credit file. Think of it as an IRS account number.

An EIN can be obtained over the phone once you have your incorporation documents available to fax over. You can also download the form from the IRS website or call them on the phone. You are more likely to receive relatively prompt service by calling the least busy IRS office you can find. There are several throughout the country, and if I had to take a guess, I would think that the offices in say New York or Delaware receive more calls than ones in the Kansas or Louisiana.

Incorporation

Incorporation usually provides you with a lower tax rate and some liability coverage. The lower tax rate is meant to encourage reinvestment of your money in your business. The liability coverage is meant to protect the personal assets of a small business owner so that they feel comfortable taking the risks necessary to run a business.

Filing

Print out the incorporation forms from your selected state's division of corporation's website. An incorporation document isn't much more than a name and address form that you sign and mail to the government with a check.

In addition to your name, your businesses' name and address, you will have to know what tax status you want. One option is where all of the business' profits are taxed at your personal income rate. Another is where all profits are taxed at the federal corporate tax rate which is usually lower than a personal tax rate.

Incorporating out of State

A number of years ago, Delaware and Nevada, among others, wanted to encourage business investment in their states, by offering a lower local and state tax rate for businesses. While this is not necessarily the case anymore, because so many businesses have incorporated and gone to court there, there is a court ruling on nearly every business situation. If you were in a situation similar to one where a decision had been made, both you and the courts could rely on the previous decision.

Non-profits

Non-profits are corporations whose primary purpose is not to make a profit, and include institutions such as foundations and charities. These corporations aren't allowed to have shareholders and are limited in their ability to compensate executives.

Non-profit does not automatically mean tax-exempt. Non-profit corporations can also be tax exempt but must serve some charitable purpose and receive tax exempt status by filing a request with the IRS after the incorporation documents are filed.

Partnerships

Limited partnerships include managing partners and their investors who have no control over the operations of the company. Limited partnerships share financial risk among members, but decision making authority is retained by the managing members.

Sole Proprietorships

As an alternative to Incorporation, if there won't be any employees other than the owner, a small business can choose to register a "Doing Business As" (DBA) Certificate with the County Clerks Office. A DBA certificate means a person has government approval to use a name other than his or her own when conducting business.

Risks

If a corporation misses annual maintenance payments for a period of time, it may lose its incorporation status and legal protection for its owners.

Business Cards & Letterhead

Design

For design ideas, get together business cards and letters that you've received, and look online at the websites of business card and letterhead printers to see samples. Make note of what you like in each design and use those ideas to sketch the layout of your own business cards and letterhead. If you have a short phrase that indicates what your business does or would encourage contact, include that.

If your company has an existing template for business cards, it may still be possible to make minor modifications to the template while maintaining consistency with the corporate image.

Given that a business card will often be one of the components of a first impression, having a secretary or assistant order them is a little like having him or her dress you before you meet with prospective clients.

For information on having business card printed, see the chapter on Production.

Letterhead

To keep a consistent style, it may be best to design your letterhead at the same time as you design your business cards. It is often better to store your letterhead in an electronic form than printing out a large supply so that it is not damaged in storage. If you prepare promotional materials and need letterhead, you will be able to have that printed at the same time that the promotional materials are printed.

Entrepreneurs

In building out a new business, new people are joining and titles may not be firm, so you may want to wait until a business has matured to add titles to business cards.

Healthcare

Provider Selection

The Department of Health in most states provides a yearly report on each of the health insurance providers in their state along with the number of people enrolled and the number complaints filed with the state.

Getting price quotes for health insurance can be done much in the same way you would search for insurance price quotes for your car. You can use online quote request forms either at the websites of individual health care providers, which can be found through an internet search, or of course over the phone.

When choosing a health insurance provider, do not rely on the marketing materials, read the actual contract, as the marketing materials may misrepresent what is actually being provided to you.

Monthly Payments

All you really need to send every month is a check with your account number clearly written on it. If the insurance company cashes your check before its due date, and your account number is clearly written on it, they have a legal obligation to provide services. To further protect yourself, you can also pay significantly in advance and submit payment through a wire transfer or online bill payment service as independent verification the money was sent.

Referrals & Reimbursement

Many health plans require that you have a referral from your primary care physician before you see any other doctor. A primary care physician is a physician who has an agreement with your health insurance provider to accept their insurance, and who you designate as your primary physician with the health insurance company. If you a see a doctor without a referral when one is required, it is unlikely your insurance provider will reimburse you.

More expensive health care plans sometimes do not require that you have a referral from your primary care physician, and will still cover a significant portion of your bill if you see doctors who do not accept your insurance.

To be reimbursed for expenses that your health insurance provider covers but you paid for yourself, you will need to submit a claim reimbursement form which can be downloaded from a healthcare provider's website, as well as faxed or mailed to you.

To be reimbursed for a prescription you generally have to submit the receipt as well as a copy of the statement that was provided from the pharmacy along with your prescription.

When submitting claims for reimbursement, it may be wise to prepare multiple copies of receipts and forms as you may have to submit your request more than once.

Uninsured Costs

A healthcare provider may be willing to negotiate rates if you do not have insurance or a significant amount of your bill is not covered by insurance and you can show that you would otherwise not be able to pay. Healthcare providers have their own list of prices, but what they actually receive from health insurance companies is often significantly less.

Medical providers may also be willing to provide you with a payment plan where you pay a small portion of the bill each month until it is paid in full. If you can show that a payment plan is necessary because you otherwise can't pay, a healthcare provider is more likely to allow this.

Providers may report non-payment to the credit bureaus, which will damage your credit rating, so it's best to call them up and try to work something out.

Prescription Coverage

Prescriptions are often covered by a company other than the primary health insurance provider. Often when a suitable generic version of a prescription medication is available, health insurance will often only cover the generic version. If they do cover the brand name version of the medication, your portion of the cost will likely be higher.

Dental, Vision & Hearing

These are add-ons to basic healthcare coverage, and many employers either don't provide these benefits or provide employees the option of paying extra for them.

Elective Procedures

Procedures or services that are not medically necessary are generally not covered.

Hospitalization

Hospital visits have a higher co-payment, certain costs may not be covered and there may be a maximum amount you insurance will cover.

Secondary Insurance Coverage

Supplemental insurance coverage that you carry on your own may cover expenses not covered by your primary insurance. Generally both the primary insurance provider and secondary insurance provider will have contractual clauses that explain dual coverage.

Medicare & Medicaid

Medicare and Medicaid are designed to cover individuals over the age of 65 and individuals with certain disabilities.

Pre-existing Conditions

Many states have laws stating that, if you have a pre-existing condition that has been covered by a recent healthcare policy, any new provider is required to cover that pre-existing condition.

There are also special insurance programs for people with specific medical conditions such as cancer or diabetes, where these programs use the size of their membership bases to negotiate somewhat better pricing for specific specialty medicines and healthcare providers.

COBRA Healthcare Coverage

In 1992 a federal law was passed in response to the significant number of uninsured Americans, commonly refereed to as COBRA, which states that upon an employee's resignation or termination, he or she is required to be able to continue their healthcare coverage with their existing terms for up to 36 months, as long as they pay the monthly premium and a health plan is still offered by their employer.

An employer is required to notify an employee of this coverage option in writing upon their departure. An employee has 60 days to elect to be covered under this law. Most insurance companies will allow an employee to send payments to them directly, and this is often best for both the employer and employee. Other health care plans only allow payments to be made through the employer. If this is the case and your employer refuses to accept your payments, you can ask for assistance from the federal agency that oversees the COBRA program.

International Sales

There are a several billion consumers worldwide. While only a fraction of them might be interested in your product or service, that's still a lot of prospective buyers.

Language and currency present the most significant barriers to selling internationally. Additionally, foreign customers purchasing over the Internet often require an added sense of security. A solution to this problem is to group customers and provide a website version specifically tailored to each group.

Grouping Customers

Grouping customers by country may at first seem the most logical approach, as most countries have a dominant currency and language. However, this approach has its drawbacks. Larry Ellison, CEO of Oracle Corporation, a large provider of information management software, received a call from a major client. "Larry, we're going to be buying everything from Oracle Brazil, they gave us the best price." His response was to create a single list of prices for all clients and to post it to the main Oracle website.

Another approach could be to provide different prices for each language group. However, customers segmented by native language will produce groups of significantly different purchasing power. This may lead to extreme pricing discrepancies for the same product or service. Additionally, many people are able to understand two languages well enough to check out other offering prices, and feel either favored or alienated.

Perhaps the best solution is to have a website in each prospective customer's native language, and provide them with pricing in their native currency along with the freedom to choose another currency. Additionally, you might allow customers to lock in an exchange rate and price for a specified period of time. Investor Warren Buffet, in his NetJets fractional jet ownership program, allows customers to buy in through the Euro or Dollar, and in each case guarantees operational costs for a period of one year.

Currencies

To profitably accept a currency, adjustments for projected upcoming changes in its value must be included in the selling price. This can be done crudely by looking at trends on a historical price chart and making a simple projection. These price charts are freely available at many of finance sites on the Internet. Also, you may want to account for known economic and political factors. If you guarantee prices or exchange rates at the time of purchase for a period of time, and think a currency will drop in value over that period, make sure to price your services above the exchange rate. Once you have figured out where the currency is likely to move in the next year, make sure that that your price still leaves you with a profit margin within an acceptable range if the currency fluctuates, and that the price is reasonably comparable to your other prices. For companies with a substantial international sales volume, locking in exchange rates through currency swaps with an investment bank might make sense.

Languages

Selling products in another language is more easily done than providing services. Doing business in one or more foreign languages requires an accurately translated site for at least two reasons: (1) a sloppily translated site will not provide sales that justify its cost; (2) there can be legal implications. This is especially true for contracts. Any contract must include a clear and precisely translated native disclaimer, stating something like "This translated document is provided for your convenience. Only the original English version of this document is binding."

To start selling products or services in another language, first, get a computer translation of relevant documents. Free online computer translators are available on the Internet, and can be easily found through an Internet search. You can either copy and paste text directly into the translator, or provide the address of a web page to be translated.

Second, fix obvious errors and omissions such as capitalization, punctuation, and un-translated words. Machine translators usually leave in place words that were not translated. These words may be translated accurately when reentered individually into the same translator.

Third, each translation should be revised by a native speaker. If you don't have someone in the company who is a native speaker, there are a number of services that can be found on the Internet that offer the human translation of documents.

International Sourcing

Jobs that are not culture or location specific can likely be done for less money somewhere else. Outsourcing non-core components of your business allows time to be spent on other opportunities.

Finding Suppliers

The objective is to find the lowest cost while maintaining quality. You can begin your search for companies to work with online. Using a search engine, enter basic search terms in order of importance, such as "print China service", "India call service" or "Asia software develop". Because "develop" is contained in the words "development" and "developer" you will get more results. In addition to looking through individual companies, you may want to search for and look through directories that list foreign companies looking for work. Companies actively advertising in those directories may be the most responsive to your requests. Along the way, build a list with contact information. Then send out a brief email to prospective contractors to assess interest. You may see that some of the outsourcing companies already list your competitors as clients.

Make as many contacts as possible, and keep making contacts until you have found a suitable partner. When choosing an international outsourcing partner, you need someone with proven results in delivering whatever it is you're asking for. There are too many other barriers, and unforeseen problems that will come up, and your ability to control or influence these problems will not be as great as if the outsourcing partner were within reasonable commuting distance.

Because communications problems can cost money, key contacts at any outsourcing partner must be highly responsive and effective communicators. If a prospective vendor is not particularly responsive, they may not be interested or have the expertise and infrastructure to handle your request.

Free Trade Fosters Peace

An indirect benefit of international sourcing is that free trade fosters peace. Why couldn't the United States and England fight a war with each other, at least at any point in the foreseeable future? Interdependence. Our economies are closely integrated. Bankers in New York call on bankers in London every day and vice versa. Americans working in harmony with overseas counterparts can increase productivity while contributing to global peace and prosperity.

Intellectual Property

Copyrights protect the expression of an idea, a patent protects the idea itself, and a trademark protects a name.

Copyrights

Although a copyright is, in theory, established when a work is created, registering that work with the federal government's copyright office will establish a firm date of creation and thus ownership. If a copyright is ever challenged in court you will have to prove the date of creation.

Works that can be registered include literary works, performing & visual arts, audio recordings, and periodicals. Each type of expression requires the filing of a different form which can be downloaded from the federal copyright office. These forms are short, fairly straightforward and have a modest filing fee. In each case you will have to submit at least one copy of the expression of the work. When your documents have been received and processed, you will be mailed back a filing receipt.

Trademarks

A trademark provides the exclusive right to the use of a name for a company, product or service in the country in which it is registered. Ownership is assigned by a government to the first individual or organization to file an application.

Requirements

To receive exclusive ownership of a name, it must 1) not already be registered, and 2) not be easily confused with a previously registered name. Even if a trademark has been granted ownership, it can still be challenged in court by another business if that business can show your trademark and their trademark can be easily confused.

Developing a Name

Start by developing a list of keywords that describe your product, service or organization and matching them together. When choosing a name, keep in mind that the less a name specifies the type of business, the more work you will have to do to make people associate your product or service with the name. Conversely, the more a name specifies the type of business, the more limited you will be in using that name in the future to expand product or service offerings. Names for which there are already a large number of pre-existing businesses such as "Joe's Pizza" will not be granted a trademark.

For each of the potential names you have selected, make sure that there is an internet domain available and that the trademark hasn't already been registered. You can check with any company that registers domain names to see if the domain name you want is available, and search the online trademark database for your country to ensure the name hasn't already been registered.

Application Filing

Using the trademark registration website for your country, perform a search for your prospective trademark to see if anyone has registered it—if your prospective trademark consists of multiple words, do a search for the words individually or in small groups. Once you have found a name, fill out the application for that name on the website.

The application form is short document, requiring: (1) a very short description of the goods and or services you will be selling using this name, (2) the classification code of each type of product or service, (3) the first time it was used or when you intend to start using it, (4) your address or the address of your attorney, and (5) a one page document showing the use of the name.

The easiest way to get a description that is acceptable to the trademark office and to lookup the codes for goods or services you're providing is to lookup the registration of a competitor.

You should register your trademark in whatever countries you anticipate doing business. Countries with treaties regarding intellectual property provide some rights of protection to each other, but it's safest to acquire additional registrations in countries where you may be doing a significant amount of business.

Your application can take several months to end up in the hands of an examiner. You are generally not charged until your application starts going through the review process, and so it may be several months before your check is deposited or your credit card is charged. By the time the transaction occurs a planned expense may become an unplanned expense, and if your check bounces or credit card has expired you may have to go through the whole process again.

Patents

Patent are the written registration of an idea and are intended to encourage and retain innovation. Patents require inventors to disclose their inventions to the public for two reasons: first, so that in the event something were to happen to the inventor, the invention would not be lost; second, that ultimately the invention will become free to the public. In exchange for this public disclosure, the inventor is given the exclusive right to that invention for up to 20 years.

Commercial Value

There might not be any demand for your invention. If you are expecting to make money off of it, weigh the costs of registration with the potential profits.

Freedom to Operate

Even if you receive a patent, you may not be able to make use of your invention without violating the rights of other patent holders. For this reason, countless patents lay dormant and useless. There is even a website dedicated to listing these useless patents.

Requirements & Research

In your patent application, you will need to thoroughly explain how to recreate your invention from scratch. The explanation must be done using words and simple diagrams so that the invention is reproducible from the patent. Existing patents can be useful reference material in putting together your own patent application. Patents are available on the website of the United States Patent & Trademark Office website (http://www.uspto.gov/). You may at this point even find that your invention has already been registered.

Proof of Invention

The person who can prove that they were the first to come up with an invention will be issued its patent. This makes it critical that you are able to prove the date you came up with your invention. The old story that mailing something to yourself and not opening it establishes a date of creation does not hold up well in court for the reason that it is not terribly hard to open and reseal an envelop. What holds up a lot better is testimony under oath from a financially uninterested person. At a minimum, this testimony would need to come from a Notary Public who can be subpoenaed go to court to verify that they signed your notes on the date indicated. Ideally, you will want testimony from a financially uninterested person with some expertise in the field who has previously read and sign your notes indicating that they have read and understood your invention on a given date.

Patent Pending Status

Patent pending seems to be a widely used marketing ploy to indicate that you can't get a product or service anywhere else. To claim that something is patent pending really doesn't mean much, but it does seem to impress people who don't know better. I could mail in a patent application that contained a drawing of a foot, with an explanation that a foot has five toes, and say that I have patent pending status on a foot. My patent would literally be pending. That means that if you have a foot, let alone two feet, and use them, you would have to pay me royalties. It could take two or three years before the patent office would notify me that they can not grant exclusive rights to ownership of a foot.

Lawsuits

Though a patent may be approved, the strength and validity of a patent is not truly tested until it goes to court. You're only paying the patent office a few hundred or few thousand dollars to examine your patent.

If it can be shown that your invention can not be recreated from your patent, that someone else it invented before you, or is so obvious that it shouldn't have been issued a patent, your patent may be revoked. Considering that any decent patent could be at a minimum worth hundreds of thousands of dollars, it is possible that an unethical big business that feels threatened may spend substantial resources challenging your patent.

Leadership & Decision Making

"Be the change you want to see in the world."

Mahatma Ghandi

Leadership

Great leaders are as rare as great marathon runners. However, everyone is a leader in some capacity at some point in their career, and most people could be more effective in their leadership roles. Becoming a more effective leader requires a disciplined commitment to introspection, learning and personal growth.

To the extent that great leaders are made and not born, once you consciously identify the attributes and conduct of great leaders throughout history, it becomes easier to develop these attributes in yourself. And when identifying potential leaders for an organization, a historical study of leadership qualities can be used to identify people who possess the attributes found in great leaders.

Attributes

Courage & Intelligence

A leader is a decision maker and effective decision making requires courage and intelligence. When I use the word courage I do not mean to be fearless, but to be aware of fear and still act when doing so makes sense. And by intelligence I mean only raw intellectual processing power. Courage and intelligence enable the other components of effective decision making and leadership, and allow a person to:

- collect and analyze all of the information necessary to make the best decision possible
- make connections between pieces of information, and recognize when connections can't be made because of insufficient information
- recognize and confront assumptions
- recognize and confront misinformation and the people who provide it
- get information directly from the source
- listen to people who disagree and thoughtfully consider their reasoning
- foresee how decisions affect options in the future
- identify and address problems directly and immediately
- act when doing so makes sense

Honest, Straightforward & Candid

Effective leaders address problems openly, directly and immediately. They encourage the search for solutions, opportunities and development through open and honest two way communication. Ineffective leaders make assumptions and have unspoken thoughts, secrets and confidences. They create an environment that discourages open and honest debate and dialogue that would otherwise bring an organization's collective resources to bear in exposing and solving problems and maximizing opportunities.

A leader sets the tone of an organization, and a leader who is honest, straightforward and candid creates an environment where people have an opportunity to learn from mistakes, improve upon shortcomings and get the support necessary to succeed.

While being candid is critically important, it's often best to reserve candor for things that are consequential and to be candid in a way that is minimally offensive. If you are candid in a way the damages communication in a relationship, then net impact of your help will be negative, because you will not have a relationship in the future where you will have opportunities for candor.

Being honest, straightforward and candid prevents relationships from being damaged because decisions are not made off of assumptions or false information.

Withholding relevant and important information from someone is one step from lying and will erode trust, not just with the person who you did this to but with anyone who is aware of it.

Reliable & Trustworthy

Effective leaders are able to develop and retain supporters because they can be trusted to keep commitments. Always keeping commitments requires an understanding of the process required to make and keep commitments and the courage, intelligence and discipline to manage that process.

When making commitments, only tell someone you're going to do something when you're going to do it, not when you intend to do it. If you intend to do something then clearly state that you intend to do it but won't guarantee it. This is true even with what might seem like inconsequential commitments. If you tell someone you'll call them back right away, and you do a couple of days later, you're building up a record of not keeping commitments, and future commitments may not be considered reliable. If you use the word "intend" or "plan" rather than "will" it may spark a debate which will allow reservations to surface as well as see how important a commitment is.

If you practice making and keeping small commitments, it will help you develop a discipline that can be applied to keeping larger commitments. Additionally, if you continually build up trust by making and keeping small commitments, people will become willing to trust you with bigger things.

While it's important to keep all commitments, the more important a commitment the more damaging it is to not keep. If it becomes truly necessary to break your commitment, make sure that this is clearly, directly and immediately communicated to the other person and explore options that would satisfy them. If you find that it becomes necessary to break commitments with any frequency, you may need to develop your planning skills, as well as use the words "intend" more and "will" less.

If you don't keep your commitments, it gives you no right to hold people to theirs, because you have established that the relationship will be one of intentions. A practical consequence of this is if you shake with a customer on a sale, but have not returned his last 4 calls when you said you would, what right do you have to hold the customer to his word on the sale you think you just closed?

Vision and Passion

A leader energizes followers by creating a sense of purpose through a vision that they are passionate about. If you're not excited about doing what you're doing, how are you going to get other people excited about it? If people can sense your passion for and commitment to a vision, it encourages them to join you. And practically speaking, achieving people's emotional commitment to their work is less expensive and more effective than trying to pay for it.

It can be difficult to motivate people if they don't understand how what they're working on is an important part of a bigger picture. Identifying and articulating a vision can be aided by studying what's happening in the world now, what has happened in the past and the possibilities for the future.

The best way to have vision and passion is to allow it to happen naturally by identifying and exploring things you are passionate about and pursuing projects and work assignments that build on your passions.

Authenticity

When you are genuine with people, they are more likely to be genuine with you, which can help to develop open communication, understanding, trust and commitment. To increase your ability to genuine with people, it helps to know and become comfortable with yourself by constantly analyzing your own strengths and weaknesses. Additionally, identifying your weaknesses allows you to supplement deficient skills with personal development and people.

Resilience & Tenacity

Leaders can get kicked in the stomach, get back up and keep going. Theodore Roosevelt was once shot in the chest on his way to a speech. Rather than immediately seek medical attention, he continued on to give the speech he had planned, lasting over an hour.

Decision Making

Cost, Benefit & Opportunity Analysis

When making a decision, a good way to begin is to list all of the known and potential short-term and long-term benefits and costs for each available opportunity, to determine if a given opportunity is the best allocation of your resources. For any course of action, the likely benefits should outweigh the likely costs, and the opportunity should be the best allocation of your resources.

Advisors

When making important decisions it is often a good idea to make sure your thinking has been reviewed independently, critically and objectively by an advisor. Talk with the people who your decision would impact as well as people independent of the situation. Have the courage to face the truth, and deal with things as they are, and collect information from relevant sources directly.

Advisors can also have an unintentionally undisclosed even subconscious pre-existing bias or interest in the outcome which should be accounted for when considering advice. And what may work well for someone else may not work well for you or your organization. It may be nearly impossible to provide advisors with access to the same nuanced information as you have. For these reasons, it is important to limit the impact an advisor has on your decision making. You have to live with your decision, your advisor does not.

Decisions are filtered through whether you and your advisors are good people or bad people, which I define as whether you naturally feel energized helping people or hurting people. If you feel good hurting people, please take yourself out of a position where you have an impact on others.

Independent Judgment

The validity of anyone's ideas should be judged based on the ideas themselves, and not on someone's educational or employment background, so that you don't end up attributing value to bad ideas and discounting good ones. As educational institutions go, probably 99.9% of the greatest men in history didn't even go to college. I wouldn't discount Abraham Lincoln's advice because he had only 18 months of schooling or give extra weight to advice from George Bush because he graduated from two highly regarded educational institutions. And as employers go, Socrates was habitually unemployed and Ralph Waldo Emerson farmed peas by a pond, yet I wouldn't discount the advice of each. Substantial damage can be done by adopting ideas based on their source rather than their value. Ultimately use your own judgment, and if an idea makes sense, adopt it, if it doesn't or you don't fully understand it, don't.

Historical Awareness

There is an old saying that those who do not study history are doomed to repeat its failures. People read either to expand or justify their decision making. People without courage seek out writers and philosophers they agree with to justify their opinions, while people with courage seeks out all writers and philosophers and try to understand them. For every decision you will ever have to make, a substantially similar one has been made somewhere in history and has likely recorded in a book where you can look up the results of that decision.

Ideology

Often, for people to do bad things, they have to believe that what they're doing is good. They may be following an ideology, religious or philosophical, that they allow to override their own judgment and independent thinking.

Imitation without Understanding

People succeed because of some behaviors and in spite of others. When some people see a person who is very successful and see that that person is a petty liar, some people might imitate their entire set of behaviors, not taking the time to understand each and its overall impact. If you took that same person and removed the pettiness and lies, he or she may have been many times more successful.

Imitation out of Context

Recognize your operating environment. What may have worked for Nietzsche or a dictator in Africa may not be applicable in a capitalistic democracy. If you're in America in the 21st century, and order your workers to produce 1 million of the same type of shoe because you read that it worked well for a period in Russia in the 90's, things may not work out.

Intellect and Instinct

At the end of the information collection and analysis process, you have two decision making tools, your intellect and your instinct. Instinct has had thousands of years to develop and an educated intellect can encompass knowledge developed throughout human history.

Intellect and instinct are both important factors. When they disagree, you have to work to understand why. When the two agree, a decision has usually been made.

Lies

"A lie can travel halfway around the world, while the truth is still putting on its' shoes"

Mark Twain

Lie based techniques are sometimes used by people who can't get ahead based on their abilities so instead use lie based techniques to tear others down. Lies based techniques never create value, but instead destroy or transfer it to the perpetrator. Not allowing lie based techniques to enter a decision making process, allows for promotion and responsibility to be assigned based on performance and will put people in place that will allow an organization to achieve optimal performance. In this section I list lie based techniques used to distort the decision making process, followed by the process to counter them. I only list these techniques so that they can be identified, exposed, neutralized, and the offenders held accountable. They should never be used.

The Confidential Informant

The Confidential Informant plants lies by requiring you to keep the lie secret before it is disclosed. The Confidential Informant will say they have something to tell you but that it has to be told in confidence because they are worried what might happen if the target finds out and may even make you think you'll be subjected to legal liability or an attack if you disclose the lies. If you agree to hold something in confidence before being told it, you become a pawn, because your thinking may change, but it would require that you compromise your honesty and trustworthiness if you were to determine the truth of what was told in confidence. This technique can be used to take someone out who knows that the Confidential Informant has engaged in illegal or unethical behavior. This technique only works with the participation of you as an accomplice. If you allow this technique to be used on you, you're helping the person who's hurting you and emboldening them to take future action against you. If you are going to let a piece of information enter your thought process, you have to directly and candidly confront its validity, or not let it change your thinking at all.

The Protector

The Protector creates and manages artificial conflicts to create the perception of indispensability while increasing compensation and or power. The Protector creates the perception of looking out for the boss and organization by falsely informing the boss that the Protector's target is plotting against the boss or organization. This technique is most effective when the Protector cuts off communication between the target and boss by creating paranoia and distrust. Others may even backup the Protector out of fear. The net impact is that organizational morale is diminished, while losing the productivity of employees taken out, and the resources required to both replace them and manage the artificial conflicts. The Protector wants to be able to say "we've been through war together and I've been loyal to you the whole time."

The Proxy

The Proxy technique involves hiring people who operate in a way that is illegal or unethical, providing them resources and encouragement to act in that way, and then claiming not to know anything when they operate in as planned, encouraged or instructed. If caught, the Proxy will claim they were only acting as told, so they're not accountable, and the Proxy Controller will claim they're not accountable because it was the Proxy. If the Proxy Controller is confronted about the Proxy's activities, not only will he or she will claim no knowledge but say that you should have spoken up sooner, to create the perception of not being responsible while making you seem accountable. This technique can be used internally or externally through lawyers, consultants and private investigators.

The Detective

The Detective creates and then finds evidence of misconduct. The only thing this is evidence of is the Detective's fraud. This is more commonly known as a setup. The detective may have his evidence recorded by an independent party to create the perception of legitimacy. The Detective routine may be used when the Detective has done something illegal or unethical and wants to take out those who might say something. This technique is most effective when the accused is not aware of the accusation and or not allowed the opportunity to fully confront the claims. The Detective has to make it look like they believe the target has done something wrong, spending significant resources creating evidence and pursuing the target as if he or she has done something wrong, in order to be able to say, "Why would I go to all of this trouble if I didn't believe it?"

The Insulator

The Insulator makes himself the person the boss gets his information from by making it easiest to get information from him or her than letting the boss collect it. This allows the Insulator to block people from informing the boss about the insulators misconduct or from forming relationships with the boss.

The Ventriloquist

The Ventriloquist communicates information while making it sound as though it's coming from someone else. This may be done when this person knows the recipient won't like something they have to say. The Ventriloquist will tell the boss they naturally don't agree with what has been said, but just wanted to be helpful and pass the information along.

The Advocate

The Advocate creates the perception of advocating on behalf of someone else, while actually advocating on their own behalf at the expense of that person. This can be done by entering a negotiation on someone's behalf when the Advocate is ultimately looking to negotiate something for him or her self with the boss in the future. To be prepared for his or her own negotiations, the Advocate can use different scenarios on the boss to determine reactions while creating the impression the Advocate is loyal to the boss by portraying the target as disloyal.

The Leech

The Leech is someone of limited talent who attaches him or her self to someone who does have talent while creating the perception of contributing to this persons work when in fact the Leach is taking away from it. The Leach may say the person they've attached to is good but need to be managed or may extol the value of being a big picture thinker in order to take the focus off the fact that they do not have the skills necessary to contribute in a meaningful way.

The Agreeable

The Agreeable creates the impression that he or she will do something deadline sensitive for the target but intentionally doesn't follow through in order to leave the target damaged.

Competence Attack

The competence attack is based on asking a target a question outside of their area of expertise, in front of the boss or witnesses, that the boss incorrectly perceives as being within the target's subject area in order to discredit the technical competence of the target. The attacker will then tell boss the question and the answer, and how someone who is technically competent could not have answered that way. Additionally, the attacker then appears technically competent, when in fact they may have had to research the question for the setup. This increases the perceived value of the attacker and decreases the perceived value of the competent employee.

Redirected Blame

This occurs when an employee lets his boss know the boss did something wrong instead of going to his boss's boss, but the boss then goes to his boss and tells him the employee did something wrong. A variation on this technique is when a person has done something wrong, and brings the problem to his boss's attention, telling him he doesn't know who caused the problem, but thinks it's his target.

Misdirection

Misdirection is putting emphasis on an issue that is controversial and substantially irrelevant, which is an admission by the misdirector that they will lose on what's relevant. The misdirector may take something said or done out of context harping on how inappropriate it was when there isn't actually a problem when placed in context with details. Misdirection works to create an image of someone that can be disliked or guilty of something so that attacks can be justified and to bring others in to participate.

Timed Lie

The Timed Lie technique is used to make sure there is insufficient time to determine what's being said is false. This technique relies on the thinking that if someone yells fire, there must be smoke, when in fact the Timed Lie is an admission that there isn't even smoke.

The Hit and Run

The Hit and Run is when someone initiates a conflict in private and then when they are recording the conversation through email, instant messenger, a call recording, or with witnesses, completely switches to being warm and friendly, to portray you as the attacker if you respond to their previous attacks. They will try to catch you unaware and use your response to increase their attacks claiming their attacks are done out of self-defense.

Kicking the Dog

Kicking the dog is when you knowingly take action against someone innocent simply to create the perception of solving a problem. This can be done to maintain control, passive-aggressively threaten others, or because the perpetrator is afraid of taking action against the real guilty person. This does not resolve the problem, it just makes you a bad person.

Discrimination

The only cover for discrimination is for the perpetrator to make it look like he or she believe the person being discriminated against has done something wrong. Discrimination damages the productivity of organization by consuming resources from the perpetrator, the victim and the organization. Treating minority employees fairly increases their loyalty in a way that can not be done with non-minority employees, and may attract minority candidates for employment who might be of a higher caliber than candidates you would otherwise be able to attract.

The Dummy

The Dummy pretends to not see wrongdoing, so that they don't have to say anything about it and can't be held accountable later for not saying anything. They may even help the perpetrator go after any person who does have the courage to say something.

The only thing more despicable and cowardly than not speaking up in the first place is attacking those who do speak up. Edmund Burke once wrote "The only way for evil to prevail is for good men to do nothing." Elaborating on that idea, if good men who do speak up are left to be attacked, evil can also prevail.

The Accomplice

This is the most insidious and despicable technique. It is the technique upon which all other techniques rely. The accomplice is you – if you allow any of the above lie based techniques to be used, as they can not work without you. Embrace courage and decency over fear and apathy. You should turn on the person using these techniques not the person they are being used on.

You are naive if you think that someone who uses these techniques will use them on everyone but you. People who use these techniques, even if not directly on you at first, will use them on you at some point – they're going to get you too, so you might as well stand up to them sooner rather than later.

Weakening Techniques

While these are not lie based techniques, it seems incomplete to not include them here. Weakening techniques include cutting your project from the budget, reassigning responsibilities, setting up arbitrary and impossible performance requirements, assigning menial responsibilities in addition to regular responsibilities, exclusion from important meetings to prevent optimally performance of duties and ultimately and covertly hiring a replacement.

Innuendo

Innuendo is used to imply something is true without explicitly saying that it's true, when in fact the premise of the implication is a lie. This can take the form of repeating accusations as fact, perhaps while even being the person who made the initial accusations. The wording on this technique can be "I wouldn't say x, but I'd say y" where x is what the lie the person wants you to believe, and y is the watered down version of the lie.

Credibility

Some people believe that if they work to artificially create and artificially destroy the perception of credibility, they can make their lies true and make the victims truths seem like lies. This is based on the idea that perceptions are reality. In the short term perceptions may be reality, but not the long term.

When a liar is confronted they may call unfavorable facts "outrageous" or "serious allegations" in order to create the perception of discrediting them while later being able to say if the evidence shows them to be indisputable true they didn't say they weren't true.

Isolation

If someone is successfully removed with any of these techniques, the person who removed them will work to block anyone else from contact with that person, so that they are not found out. If information sources are being cut off, your leader may not be acting in your best interests. Because conflicts can not be resolved without communication, lawyers will sometimes use this technique to increase their fees.

Countering Lies as the Victim

The general counter to a lie based technique, when you can find out one is being used, is to explain the technique to whoever it's being used on, provide the truth, and explain the damage the technique does to the organization. If you suspect a lie based technique, you can ask if something is not being said because it was told in secret by saying something like "has anyone provided any negative information about me?" and "if this person is lying to you would you want to know?" Some people really don't want to know that they're being lied to and will fight to defend the lie they've been told, especially if they have already acted on the lie and would be potentially damaged if they admitted they did the wrong thing.

Countering Lies as the Decision Maker

Countering lies as the decision maker requires the courage and intelligence to recognize and confront these techniques and the people who use them. Don't make a decision without having the courage, intelligence and decency to ask the accused directly. If you trust the source, that's even more reason to verify, because people can take advantage of that either maliciously or by being lazy in not properly and fully disclosing the information you would need to make an informed decision. You will set yourself up to get false or misleading information if people know that you are the type to not to directly disclose and discuss information with the accused.

If someone claims to be worried about repercussions and must tell you something in confidence, tell them you can't promise that you will keep the information secret but will promise that if told in good faith will do everything possible to make sure that there aren't any consequences.

When someone presents negative information about someone else, a simple question to ask, though never a replacement for asking the accused directly, is "what would this person tell me if they were here right now?"

It never ceases to amaze me when I see one person get angry at another based on something they were told without talking with the accused, when often they should not be angry at the accused but furious with the person who provided the information.

Without directly confronting these techniques, you will be making assumptions based on lies, which is the best way to make a disastrous decision.

To the people who already use these techniques, you only get a shot time on this earth – is it really worth being an awful person to become successful? In the context of an infinite universe that has always been and will always be, where we were preceded by the dinosaurs and will be succeeded by something else, and we have the technology to cause our own extinction, I can't see meaning or value in doing anything other than helping others while still enjoying your own life. Succeeding while lying, cheating, stealing, hurting others seems like a terrible and misguided way to spend life and maybe you should be doing something else.

I conclude this section on Decision Making reminded of the words of the comedian Chris Rock when he was talking about kids who brought guns to school and shot a room full of classmates. "Everyone wants to know what kind of music was they listening to, what kind of movies

they was watching. Forget the music. Forget the movies.
Crazy. What, you can't be crazy no more?"

Marketing

Effective marketing involves developing an advertisement and selecting a medium that will provide the lowest cost per sale.

Development

Collect advertisements of competitors, and make a list of what might appeal to customers. Then compare what is being offered to what you offer. Finally, rework your advertisement to be a compelling choice when compared with competitors while still being consistent with your product or service.

Response & Conversion Rates

After you have designed one or more advertisements, test the response rate. After you find the most successful advertisement, you can refine it one step further and prepare and test variations of that advertisement.

The easiest place to test the response to an ad is online. You can see how many times the ad was viewed and how many times it was clicked on. This response rate should give you a better idea of what the response rate will be in other advertising mediums.

While the number of respondents is important, the number of those respondents that actually turn into customers is most important. One way to determine this is to place the advertisements online at different times and review website visitor logs to see where visitors who placed orders came from.

Targeting & Publication

Once you have selected a final advertisement, spend a small amount to run the advertisement in a few magazines, newspapers, websites, and mailing lists. Determine which of those provides you with the highest response rate per dollar spent, and run the advertisement in the amount you have budgeted accordingly.

Income Projections

To project income for a marketing campaign, take the amount you plan to spend, the number of responses that amount will generate, and the number of responses that turn into sales, and the average total profit per sale. These were the numbers you previously obtained by testing different advertisements. If you use spreadsheet software to make these calculations, you can change one number and have it recalculate all of the other numbers.

Mediums

Internet

Online advertising programs will typically charge per display or per click. Determining which is most cost effective depends on how frequently people click on your advertisement. Online advertising programs regularly come and go so rather than list them here it may be best to find them through Internet search for something like "online advertising programs".

Internet advertising also allows you to take advantage of social networks which enable people to easily share whatever you're marketing with their online social networks. If you can design your product or service in such a way that it's something people want to tell their friends about, it can then spread partly on it's own through social networks.

Running an advertising campaign online is like being a conductor. As the campaign runs, reallocate budgets to sources that offer the lowest cost per sale.

Magazines & Newspapers

Get the phone numbers for the advertising director of magazines that you think your customers read and request that they mail out rate information. There are typically different rates for the print and online versions of magazines and newspapers.

Radio & Television

The cost of radio and television advertising depends largely on the size of the audience that it will be presented to. Radio & T.V. stations should be able to provide you with an approximate audited count of listeners and or viewers at different times and for different programs. Advertisement time is usually sold in blocks of 30 or 60 seconds.

Some radio stations will for an additional fee record your advertisement with a professional actor. Before you do this, record a rough draft of your advertisement on your computer, and either ask the radio station to re-record it or find a recording studio. If you find your own recording studio, be sure to get the audio file format specifications from the radio station before recording.

Producing a television commercial can begin with a script you write yourself and a rough home made video of what you're looking to create, which can then be emailed out to production companies to solicit bids to produce a professional version.

Direct Mail

Once you have created a piece of mail you would like to send out, you have the option of paying bulk rate or first-class rate for postage. Bulk postage rates are great for magazines whose subscribers have already ordered, or newsletters by paid members. If you will be regularly sending out a large quantity of mail, you may want to apply for a bulk mail permit from the U.S. Postal Service. With bulk mail, you receive a discount if your mail is sorted by zip code, because it is easier for the post office to get it started on the way to its final destination. When your import your address book into a label printing program, make sure to arrange addresses in ascending order by zip code.

However, a bulk postage stamp indicates a mass mailing which may make your envelop less likely to be opened. There seems to me a psychological difference between receiving a piece of mail that has a hand placed first class stamp and one that is labeled bulk postage paid.

Trade Associations

If you are a member of a trade group or the local chamber of commerce, it could be to your benefit to include that association in your marketing materials. The Better Business Bureau (http://www.bbb.org/) maintains records on registered businesses including a public database of complaints against any registered business. These complaints may be filed by any person or organization that has done business with the company. They require a business to provide proof it has been in existence for at least one year before applying for membership, and it would be very difficult to provide the documentation required by the BBB without being a legitimate business.

Promotional Items

Promotional items can be an inexpensive way to build your brand, commemorate an achievement, or build momentum for the launch of a product or service.

Selection

The best promotional items are ones that someone would use every day, as they keep your company on a person's mind for a limited amount of money. People keep for years items such as embroidered jackets, backpacks, bags, key rings and coffee mugs.

Production

There are many companies that can be found with a quick internet search that will embroider your logo into clothing or other small promotional items. You can even buy your own clothing and search for a company that will embroidered it. Its best to ask for samples of previous work, and ideally a single sample of your item before the rest are produced, as that is the best way to ensure that you end up with what you want. For additional information on the production of promotional items, see the chapter on Production.

Networking

There's an old expression that it's now what you know it's who you know. To the extent that that's true, what's even more true is that it's not who you know, but what they're willing to do for you. When building a network it's important to work on becoming someone people want to help, and one of the ways to make that happen is to always look for ways to be helpful to others.

Friends & Family

Most friends of friends and family are usually willing to be helpful when all they're asking for is time and knowledge. If you're looking to do a deal, and a person has only offered time and knowledge you have to work on building a relationship first.

Professional Associations & Events

Trade associations and chambers of commerce host events including speakers and breakfasts. Networking events can be a relatively inexpensive and time efficient way to meet prospective customers, employees and investors, get face to face feedback on your products or services, and meet the competition.

Association members can also serve as an informal peer support group. A fellow association member may be more likely to lend their time and relevant expertise to you. You can almost always use the organization's seal on corporate communications, subject to guideline compliance, to show that you are a part of the community. Many trade associations maintain a public membership directory for members to develop cross promotions and receive discounts.

To find professional associations, look at the associations that already represent your competitors. Additionally, industry trade publications will usually contain advertisements for various professional organizations. Subscribing to some relevant industry publications will help keep you aware of relevant upcoming events and new offerings of competitors.

Preparing for Events

If possible, go through mock approaches with a colleague, spouse or friend. Have your company's background and your personal background down cold and make a list of questions you think you might get along with accompanying answers. If you can't go through a mock practice session, practice saying everything you might say at the event out loud many, many times before you show up. It may not be wise to let the event to be the first time you practice your presentation.

Meeting People at an Event

The purpose of making new contacts at an event is to begin relationships that you can follow-up on later. It's unlikely that you're going to walk up to someone you don't know and make a sale, and pursuing that objective will detract from the objective of building a relationship that you can follow-up on.

Have a plan for moving between people. If initiating contact is the most difficult thing to do at a networking event, breaking contact is the second most difficult. It's easy and comfortable to get bogged down talking with a single person. As a rough guide as to how much time to spend with any give person, decide how many people you want to meet at the event, and figure out how much time you can spend with each person given the duration of the event. If you go over that time because you are engaged in conversation with a good prospect that's fine, but if you're about to hit that time and are sticking with this person simply because it's more comfortable than the alternative of going out to talk with others, move on.

As some point, even if you're having a decent conversation, let the person know you'd like to continue talking, hopefully later on at the event, but that you want to exchange contact information before moving on.

If you join a group of people, you have to contribute to moving the existing conversation forward, and engaging all participants, before changing or altering topics. If you haven't done the former before the latter, you will likely be ignored.

If you're new to trade events in the community and you meet someone who goes to events regularly, it may be a good idea to engage that contact and see if they might let you tag along with them to other events.

Organization

Identify Priorities & Create a Task List

Identifying personal and professional priorities is an introspective process. Once you have identified your priorities, identify each of the tasks necessary to achieve those priorities. Every task should be an action and include a priority level, estimated time, energy and cost. If you can't come up with time, energy and cost for a task, then it hasn't been clearly defined, or needs to be broken down into smaller tasks.

Time & Energy

It's not how much time something takes, its how much energy it takes. It may be possible for something like a conference call with your biggest customer to take your productive energy for the morning even though it was fairly brief. When adding energy estimate to each task, work off of having 1 unit of energy every day, so that when you add time and energy to a task it might look like the sample task list below.

Sample Task List

Priority	Method	Contact	Description	Time	Energy	Cost
1	Phone	Bob	Order fee	15 M	.15	
1	Internet	Staples	Order pens	10 M	.01	$20

Stress

There are two types of stress: productive stress and unproductive stress. Stress that helps you be productive is positive in moderation, while stress that does not help you be productive and only helps to take away from productivity needs to be minimized.

It can be good to regularly make a list of all stressors and look at moderating positive stress and reducing negative stress. When identifying stressors, remember that if something can not be controlled, stress is about the only thing that can result from trying to control it, and you may want to stop trying to attempt control.

Thought control can be useful in controlling stress, by not allowing unproductive stressful thoughts in your head and moderating productive stressful thoughts.

Payment Collection

Payment options should not be an impediment to customer spending, but at the same time offering too many options can incur unnecessary fees and administrative costs.

Credit Cards

To accept credit card directly you will need a business checking account, a credit-card merchant account, a transaction processor, and for retail operations; a machine to read credit cards or take an imprint.

A merchant account acts as a buffer between the when a buyer's card is charged and when funds are deposited to your account, and is intended to provide a layer of protection for buyers. A transaction processor provides what is called a "payment gateway" which is required to transmit the information between from your buyer to your merchant account. A credit card reader or imprint machine can be purchased from the provider of your merchant account or processing gateway.

American Express requires a more lengthy and rigorous application process than MasterCard or Visa, and charges a slightly higher percent of each transaction than their competitors. There are benefits to being a merchant with American express including the association with the

American Express brand, the confidence Amex buyers have in the security of their purchase, and possible listing in Amex's merchant directory.

Applying to accept credit cards can cost several hundred dollars and there are monthly maintenance fees for the business checking account, credit card merchant account, and transaction processor.

Third Party Online Processing

There are a number of online payment services such as PayPal that allow a customer to have an independent third-party be in complete control of payment processing, adding an additional layer of security that may make a buyer more comfortable and a sale more likely.

Entrepreneurs

When you're starting out, having multiple payment options is secondary to actually selling something. Once you make a couple of sales, consider expanding the payment options you offer, but focus first on your sales. You can start out by only accepting checks and once you have made your first sale then consider additional payment methods.

Invoicing

If you choose to invoice clients, go through the invoices that you have received from companies for ideas on layout and format. When invoicing clients, you can also offer a small discount for quick payment.

Collection Agencies

If a customer will not pay a legitimate bill, you can bring in a collection representative one of two ways. The first is someone who works on a fee basis to manage collection of the account, the second is to completely sell the account debt for a fraction of the amount to a collection agency.

Payroll

Payroll management is a detail oriented and time consuming process where payments must be made regularly not only to the employee directly, but indirectly to any retirement accounts, and in taxes to the state and federal governments. Unless you have a large Human Resources department, it's often best to use an outside payroll management service.

Payroll service companies will pay taxes on your behalf, directly deposit money into your employees' checking accounts, and provide pay stubs, as well as year end earnings summaries and tax forms. Some banks offer this service with a business checking account for a small additional fee. You can have an account with a bank just for payroll even if you don't do any other business with them. It's also a good idea to have a separate bank account for payroll to help ensure those funds are always available.

Paystubs

Pay stubs are a paycheck receipt, and employees will usually need pay stubs to rent an apartment, or apply for a credit card or mortgage. To provide pay stubs you can either request that your payroll service send you these in the mail or use desktop payroll software that will allow you to print them yourself.

Direct Deposit

Direct deposits electronically transfer money from your business checking account to your employees' personal checking accounts, saving you from having to print and sign checks and employees from having to deposit them.

New Employees

You will need to, on behalf of new employees, submit two federal forms: an Employment Eligibility Verification Form I-9 and an Employees Allowance Withholding Certificate W-4.

At the state level, you generally have to report a new hire within a couple of weeks of when he or she starts, which can usually be done online at the states taxation website. This is not only to give the state notice so that they can be sure you're paying taxes on the employee's income, but also to inform you if the employee's wages are to be garnished by a tax lien and to calculate state and national employment statistics.

Foreign Workers

Foreign workers are required to file for a Social Security Number. The application for a Social Security Number by a foreign worker is passed through the Department of Homeland Security to verify eligibility. If a SSN is not available at the time of submitting tax payments, check the box on the form next SSN "Applied For".

Taxes

An organization is required at the federal and state level to withhold and submit, from each paycheck, income tax and a matching amount of Social Security, Medicare, and unemployment tax. Social Security tax is due up until the employee has contributed a yearly maximum. Some states also require that you withhold and submit disability tax from an employee's paycheck.

Making Payments

In order to make required tax payments on behalf of an employee you will need his or her social security number as well as your organizations EIN (see EIN section in Formation chapter for more information).

If you will be handling payroll without the help of a service, payments can be made electronically to the federal government and most state governments through their respective websites. Each state has a Department of Taxation & Revenue or something with a similar title that can be found with a quick Internet search. There you should be able to download all of the forms you need and submit payments.

Year End

In addition to filing year end tax forms on behalf of the organization, you are required to provide each employee who paid taxes an IRS form that states the total amount of tax in each category paid on their behalf so that they can file their personal tax forms.

Retirement Account Contributions

Retirement account deposits are usually made quarterly. Statements for the account come directly from the institution that maintains the account and go directly to the employee. Contributions to retirement accounts are usually not taxed when the money is deposited but when it is withdrawn to allow it to collect additional interest. There is a maximum amount that an employee is allowed to contribute each year tax free.

Software

Some payroll services will allow you to manage services from a web browser or provide desktop software. There are also a number of payroll software packages which can be found with an Internet search that are compatible with most payroll management services.

Non-Profits

Non-profits are still liable for contributing payroll taxes because services such as tax funded programs for unemployment and disability are available to employees of non-profits just are they are for-profits.

Pricing

Pricing can be based on costs, competitors' prices or perceived value. Choosing the right pricing method or combination of pricing methods is an important component of an organizations' financial success.

Cost

Cost based pricing is where you take the cost of producing your goods or services and add to it a fixed percent of the cost to get your sale price. This is often not the most profitable method and may only be viable for an organization built on operational efficiency with a dominant market position. An example of a cost based retailer is Wal-Mart, where they work to keep knocking down their costs and make money by selling large quantities.

Competitor

Competitor based pricing is simply setting your prices based on competitors' prices. This will usually allow for a healthy profit margin. However, if prices allow for an excessive profit margin, new competitors may enter and move the industry to a cost-based pricing model to undercut competitors. If that happens and prices do not allow for a reasonable profit margin, you either have to cut costs or exit the business. Airlines initially used a competitor based pricing model, but later shifted to a cost-based pricing model, lowering prices while costs remained stagnant, driving each other into bankruptcy.

Perceived Value

If you have a highly differentiated product, highly specialized skill set, or there are few competitors in your market, then your can price your products based on the value clients perceive them to have, creating a profit margin that has little relationship to costs or competitors prices. Diamond manufactures are able to do this by controlling the supply of diamonds while charging more for what are to the untrained eye unperceivable differences in quality.

Privacy Policy

A privacy policy covers the collection, use and distribution of information and can be a component of your company's brand.

There are a couple of consumer protection agencies that have respected guidelines for consumer privacy including the Federal Trade Commission and the Better Business Bureau. The BBB offers a logo that can be attached to your privacy policy upon their approval of your privacy policy. Guidelines are available on their respective websites.

Developing a privacy policy that you do not stick to or that provides for invasion of privacy may permanently damage customer relationships.

Sample Privacy Policy

This policy governs the collection, use and distribution of personal and organizational information obtained by the Company during the course of business.

Collection

We may collect the following information during any interaction:

Website Visitors: date, time, web browser, operating system and identifying address.

Individuals: name, organization, title, background, address, phone, fax and email.

Organizations: same as individuals, as well as key contacts (individuals), research and analysis

We may obtain information through publicly available documents as well as any self-reporting, email, fax, voicemail, meeting or phone call.

Use

All information obtained will be used to better serve our customers.

Distribution

We will not sell your personal information to any outside individual or organization. We may disclose information to outside parties if doing so becomes reasonably necessary in the performance of services.

Production

Producer Selection

Begin by contacting a number of printers or manufacturers in your area and maybe even some outside of the country, which can be found through an Internet search, and request samples of work done for other customers. Any printer or manufacturer that has been in business for a couple of years has excess materials lying around that they have produced for other clients. You can tell from the samples whether or not they have the skill and machinery necessary to produce what you'd like. It's important to select a printer or manufacturer who has proven through samples they can provide you with the final result you want.

Requesting Quotes

Prepare and send an electronic or physical packet to each contact. To get an accurate quote, your packet should include every single component necessary for production.

Digital Files

There are standard file formats which will be listed on the websites of the production company.

Color Matching

If you are producing something where 100% exact color reproduction is required, you will need a Paint Matching System (PMS) number for each color. These can be looked up in a PMS book which can be found at any decent size book store or at the producer's shop.

Proofs

Once you selected a producer, request that they develop and send a single finished sample, referred to as a proof. Even if you don't intend on making any changes, a proof will require the producer to ensure ahead of time that the job is done properly. If you do not request a physical proof it is unlikely that you will get exactly what you want. You may think you're being gracious by not asking for the extra work necessary to create a proof, but your being a gracious when the job is done wrong, and you let it slide.

If you ask a producer to make adjustments to a file, it will rarely come out right, even for simple requests. The person managing your order and the person fulfilling it are usually different, and the middleman can be a source of miscommunication. Additionally, your producer has his own perceptions and limitations, and may have a different idea from you as to how the project is best modified.

Get a producer to commit in writing to the specifications of your project and beware of substitutions and alterations. Always have them make clear to you the specifications are exactly what you discussed before signing an agreement. If they ask you what type of material you want, respond you want whatever type you agreed on, otherwise they may try replace one material with another because it's what they had in stock.

Once you have received a satisfactory proof, ask for production to be completed.

Publicity

"The simple message always wins."
Larry Ellison
Founder, Chairman & CEO
Oracle

Publicity is the least expensive and most credible way to promote a business because it usually comes from a source with limited financial interest in your success. By contrast, advertising is the most expensive and least credible way to promote your business because anyone can pay to have their advertisement run. However, because it is usually more profitable for someone to sell you advertising than to print an article about you, it is usually more difficult to get publicity than place an advertisement.

Develop a Message

Write up an interesting story about or review of your product or service with points that could be pulled right out of the story and put into an author's article. The less work for an author or editor, the more likely they are to write about you. Keep your overall message simple and repeat it often. Your story should lead people to arrive at your conclusion without you needing to explicitly state it. Decide what single thought you want someone to take away from your story, and make sure that's the thought you leave with after reading it.

Develop Contacts

Start by collecting the magazines, newspapers, and industry publications that you think your target customers read. From there, collect articles on similar products or services, and take down the contact information of the author as well as the publication. When you have developed your message, begin making contact through emails and phone calls.

Send Out Press Releases

A press release is just a written message developed to be sent out to the media. The typical release simply includes a headline, your message, and a note at the bottom with contact information.

When it comes time to send out the press release, you can send it out through email, fax or postal mail, or through a press release service that can send your message out to recipients targeted by industry and location. To find a press release service, you can look at press releases from your competitors which will note the press release service used.

Interview

Before an article is actually published, a phone or in-person interview will often be conducted, so be prepared once the press releases go out. In preparing for an interview, look online for interviews that have been conducted on a similar topic. If you know who will be interviewing you, look at past interviews they've done if possible. Develop a list of potential questions, prepare written answers, practice them out loud without your notes, and then ask a friend or co-worker to interview you. The harder the practice interviews, the easier the real interview will be, and the more likely you will get quality publicity.

Sales

The overriding goal in sales is to make sure every action moves the relationship forward.

When identify prospects, look for people who have a need, not a desire for what you're selling. People are significantly more likely to spend money on a need than a desire. In addition to likely increasing sales, you will also be helping people if you're actually meeting a need rather than pushing products or services on them. Once you have identified prospects that need what you're selling, help prospects identify and elaborate on that need. Help them make themselves acutely aware of the problems that come from leaving that need unresolved and offer a solution.

Keep a Journal

Begin this process by starting a journal to plan and record interactions with prospects. These interactions can later be attached as notes to the prospect in your electronic contact manager. In sales, even the smallest details mentioned can be valuable later, so it is important to take detailed notes during any interaction to the extent that doing so doesn't take away from building the relationship.

Develop a Message

Create a written list of selling points for your product or service and of how you're offering compares to competitors' offerings. Look for examples and short stories that bring each selling point to life not only engage the person listening but also help that person to reach his or her own conclusions. Prepare a list of potential objections and a response to each.

Phone Calls

Write out a script in your journal that includes your opening, selling points, each of the questions that could be asked along with answers, and a closing statement.

Voicemail

If you write out a voicemail message prior to a phone call and practice it out loud, and the person doesn't pick up, you will be able to leave a message where you are prepared to say everything you want to say and hopefully avoid saying anything you didn't want to say. If they do pick up, you will know exactly what you want to talk about.

If you leave your phone number right after your name at the beginning of a voicemail message, and the recipient needs your phone number, they can repeat the message and get your number quickly. You may also want to include the day and time at the beginning of your message, as many voicemail systems don't clearly indicate when a message was left.

Practice

Perhaps most important to the success of a sales call is to practice with someone beforehand as many times as possible, and ideally once on the phone immediately before calling the prospect.

Making the Call

Do whatever you need to do to create an environment where you feel comfortable. If possible, listen to your favorite music or have your favorite movie on in the background until you're ready to pick up the phone. Make sure that you create for yourself a positive state of mind and have a smile on your face.

When talking on the phone, facial expressions and hand gestures can come across in your voice through tension or relaxation in your vocal chords, so it is important to talk as if the person were right there in front of you. A headset phone is usually best for these types of calls, because they allow you to have both hands free for natural movement.

Gatekeepers

To get past secretaries or assistants, you may have to call a number of times. If you call very early in the morning or very late in the day, the assistant or secretary might not even be there and the prospect may pickup directly. Also, it's critical that the assistant or secretary feels warmly about you, as they often have significant influence as to whether or not the prospect has time for you.

Cold Calling

The most difficult part of cold calling is dialing the phone number. Develop a one page list of names and phone numbers that you can go straight through. While it's important to keep a consistent pace, if you rush through the list you may sound rushed on the phone.

When John Whitehead, the person substantially credited with building the investment bank Goldman Sachs, started an aggressive push to recruit new corporate clients, he brought 4 people into a new business development division, took out a list of the fortune 500 companies, broke the country into 4 regions, and assigned 125 companies to each person. They began calling on the executive officers to see what services they could provide. The relationships took a long time to develop but were ultimately successful.

Meetings

Practice

There is perhaps nothing more important in being prepared to have a successful meeting than practice meetings. In preparation for the meeting, you may want to review the chapter on Speaking & Presentations.

Sponsors & Detractors

A sponsor is someone who is willing to vouch for you, and a detractor is someone who decides to work against you. Even if you meet someone only very briefly, they can easily become a sponsor or a detractor.

If you encounter someone who is hostile or aggressive, how you answer their questions can be more important than what you say. If you pick up one detractor, people who are loyal to that detractor may push for information or behavior that can be used to reinforce the detractor's claims, however untrue they may be.

The Meeting

Keep the focus on the prospects need, the problems caused by leaving that need unresolved, and your solution. Pickup as many sponsors as possible and avoid detractors. Leave the prospect with concise selling points he or she will be able to use on your behalf to sell you to others.

Listen and take a genuine interest in what the prospect is saying. If a person feels like they can talk to you and you understand them, you've established rapport, and they may be more likely to disclose information that is important and relevant to their decision making process.

It's important to identify decision makers and key influencers and communicate directly with them sooner rather than later. An initial meeting may be part of a screening process before you are offered a chance to meet with the final decision maker. If the meetings with key decision makers are brief, how they feel about you is more important than what you're selling. Some people will be more likely to buy a good product from someone they like than a great product from someone they don't like or don't know.

If you ask the prospect how they might see what you're offering fitting in with their organization, it will give them an opportunity to express not only what they like about you're offering but also to express any reservations which will give you the opportunity to address those reservations.

Closing the Sale

It is unlikely you will be present when the final decision is made, so you have to prepare your prospects with all of the information they need to close the sale on your behalf.

Speaking & Presentations

There is nothing more important than rehearsal when it comes to the public performance of either a speech or presentation.

Preparation

After you have written out your entire speech or presentation, go through it and identify the most important ideas. List these ideas, commit them to memory, and the practice your speech or presentation out loud without your notes. You may find yourself making up parts that you forgot and that's fine but keep going. Practice as if there were an audience, so that the rehearsal is uninterrupted and uncommented. Keep practicing the speech or presentation from start to finish until you are able to present without stopping while being articulate and engaging.

The audience tends to take on the emotions of the speaker. If you find your presentation dull, the audience will see it in your face and hear it in your voice. If you find it lively and engaging, that is how they will likely find it.

The longer and harder your practice sessions the easier and better the real thing will be.

Team Presentations

Work through the entire presentation, from start to finish, without any discussion or interruption by any team member, as if the audience were there. If anyone has anything to say about another team member's performance, they can make a note and say it after the practice session. When everyone finally gets their part right, do it again, then again. You'll know you've practiced enough times when you are on the verge of mutiny.

Videotaping

You will not truly know how you come across until you see for yourself. Have a video camera running during practice sessions, review the footage and take notes on things you'd like to change, add or remove.

Strategy & Negotiation

"Most people have the will to win. Few people have the will to prepare to win."

Rickson Gracie
Mixed Martial Arts Champion

When you are at point A and have identified point B, I think of a strategy as the way to flow like water down a hill from point A at the top to point B at the bottom. There may be obstacles, but a strategy is the plan to move around them and keep advancing.

Preparation

After you have made a decision as to what point B is using the process outlined in the chapter on Leadership & Decision Making, visually diagram your strategy on a timeline. Identify potential obstacles, a plan to work around each, and additional supporting resources that may be necessary for successful execution.

Supporting Resources

Emotional Reserves

Emotional reserves help provide the stamina necessary to successfully complete a negotiation or execute a strategy. These can be built up thorough the activities that promote a sense of well being. Identify activities have given you this feeling in you in the past. These may include things like time with family or close friends, a massage, meditation or even a night at a hotel. When deciding the costs of engaging in one of these activities, especially at a critical time, it is important to consider the costs of not doing so. Emotional reserves can be better retained if you have built up stamina through regular endurance building exercise.

Financial Reserves

Setup lines of credit and cash reserve accounts when you are strong and don't need them, for the times when you are not as strong and may need them. If you wait until you need money, you may find that people will not provide it or provide it on unfavorable terms, and lenders who find out may even raise rates and reduce limits on your existing credit accounts. Don't wait until you have to negotiate from a position of distress.

Key People Support

You have to have the relevant people who support you present. Discuss the situation directly with each key person and work to enlist their support. They should be adequately informed and actively voicing their support.

Alternatives

Thoroughly research your alternatives so that you know where you can and can not compromise. If you are trying to close a deal, sometimes those who might make an offer want to see that you have other offers, despite the fact that this drives up the cost of the deal for them. This may in part be so they can say internally, "we have to close now at this price so our competitor doesn't get them". Mostly though I think it plays on the psychological principle of scarcity, where people want what other people want when there is a limited quantity because they don't have the confidence and judgment to think independently. It would actually make more sense to be excited about a quality deal where there weren't any other offers, because that indicates that this person you're dealing with will be less likely to try to drive up the price up on you in future deals.

Humility

If people perceive you as arrogant it makes them work against you. Perceived arrogance enlists people against your cause and will dampen the effectiveness of your strategy. The difference between stating something with arrogance as opposed to confidence is usually the inclusion of a reference group. For example, it is perceived as arrogant to say "I could do a better job than anyone else on this", but is usually perceived as confident if you remove the reference group and say "I could do an absolutely outstanding job on this". Better yet, lay out the facts one by one to allow the listener to arrive at this conclusion themselves.

Lies & Deceptions

Lies & deceptions should not be used as part of a strategy, not only for ethical reasons but for practical reasons. If your followers see you using lies or deceptions, and they are not naive, they will realize that you are not going to use lies and deceptions on everyone but them, eroding their commitment to you and your effectiveness as a leader.

Finally, don't reveal your entire strategy in a book.

Taxes

When income exceeds expenses, you have a profit, and when you have a profit, you have to pay part of that profit in taxes to the government.

Determining & Submitting Payments

The exact percent of your profit to be paid out in taxes will be calculated as you fill out tax forms and usually comes to a total of around one-third of your profit. Taxes are required to be paid and forms filed annually as well as quarterly based on your projected profits for the year. To determine profits, prepare an Income Statement with supporting documentation as detailed in the Accounting Statements & Financial Projections section. Once you have determined your profit, download and complete relevant forms from the websites of the IRS and state taxation authority. Have your tax calculations and forms reviewed and submitted by a tax preparer that specializes in businesses of your size. Payments to the government can be debited your bank account on the date you indicate on your tax return.

Deductions

A deduction is an expense that is subtracted from your income before calculating taxes due. Contributions to federally recognized tax-exempt organizations may be deducted. Payments made on behalf of or reimbursed to employees may not be deducted if they are what the IRS calls "ordinary and necessary" during the course of business. Normal living and commuting expenses are not deductible.

Entrepreneurs

Most businesses do not have a profit in the first two years of business, and the IRS is aware of this. Also, if you have an extremely low level of income, for example you run a small business alone part-time as a hobby, you may not be required to file tax forms.

Non-Profits

For a non-profit to be tax-exempt, it must file for tax exempt status with the Internal Revenue Service. While non-profits corporations with tax-exempt status are not required to pay income tax, they are still required to file a report with the federal government on contributions that exceed a certain amount. They are also still required to pay contribute payroll taxes on employee's paychecks as non-profit employees are still able to access government sponsored services such as unemployment.

Dissolution

If your company or a subsidiary of it closes down you will need to file notice with the federal and state governments so that you are you are no longer liable for filing tax forms. Forms can be downloaded from the IRS website so that they can close out your Employer

Identification Number. Each state has a form that you can download from their website to dissolve your corporation.

Teamwork

Team Member Selection

A team is a group of relationships, and in every relationship there are people who fit together well and people who don't. Two dominant personalities fighting over control of a team detracts from getting things done, and renders each of diminished capacity. Choosing team members that are naturally compatible will help lay the foundation for a team's success.

Team Building

If you allocate time for team members to get to know each other's personal and professional backgrounds, strengths and weaknesses, what skills they would like to develop, and what role they would like to play, it will allow people to take on work they can and want to do well, increasing the total output of the team. It's important not only that the team leader has this information, but that the team members hear it from each other.

If you have an existing team and have never taken the time to do this it's never too late. It is particularly important for senior members take the initiative in this process. You will find out sooner or later what team members are not good at or interested in and it's better to find this out before they underperform or become unhappy.

Team building exercises outside of the office where members actively engage each other in a meaningful and fun way can help develop greater understanding and trust that will enhance working relationships and productivity.

Achieving Goals

Once you have a team that functions well together, figure out what you agree on and work to achieve that, rather than argue about what you don't agree on. Once the team has achieved momentum by constructively working on and achieving what everyone agrees on, it is more likely the team will be able to overcome other differences.

Diversity

Each person comes into the group with their own perceptions, background and way of thinking. These differences when properly engaged can provide a more comprehensive and thoughtful resolution to the teams tasks. As companies become more global, customer bases become more diverse, and so it would make sense to have a team that includes members with backgrounds similar to your customers.

Meetings

Dialogue must be honest, candid and reality based, because if you don't get the tough news from team members, you'll get it from your customers when they don't buy or from investors when they don't invest.

A team member should consistently contribute in a meaningful way before offering criticism. Allowing a team member to be critical without otherwise contributing, can take away from the morale and overall productivity of the team.

Leading & Delegating

Delegation only works effectively if the person delegating leads by example and takes on as much if not more work than other team members. Taking on the role of simply delegating tasks without otherwise equal participation can result in resentment and diminished team productivity.

Accountability

Each team member should support the success of other team members as much as possible while maintaining full responsibility for their own part of the project. Project tasks must be broken down into units for which an individual can be accountable. The only exception I can think of is when two people are known to work particularly well together they can share accountability for a component.

Technology

"Technology can't make a bad business good, but it can make a good business great."

Larry Ellison
Founder, Chairman & CEO
Oracle

Technology is important to every organization because technology enables productivity.

Buy, Upgrade or Build

Whatever technology you invest in, make certain it is technology employees will want to use by getting their help in choosing and or designing it. Having better technology that no one uses only leaves you with new costs. And because complexity costs resources, it is often best to use the simplest technologies possible that will allow for the company's growth.

Buy

Most software vendors say their products have the lowest total cost of ownership, which is measured as initial plus ongoing costs. The total cost of ownership in part depends on how you make use of the software. And the more complicated the technology, the more likely it will be expensive to install, develop, and maintain.

It is important to understand how well a piece of software can be integrated with other software you own or are looking at purchasing.

Upgrade

Generally, if it works keep it. However, even if your organization has done well in the past without making full use of technology, if you have competitors that have upgraded their technology, it may put you at a disadvantage.

Build

You may want to build your own software when you can add significant value over what can be bought, and when building can be done for a reasonable amount of time and money. It is important to completely understand a process before building a custom piece of software to support that process. If choose to build, see the section on Hiring Developers in the Employees chapter.

Collaboration

Sharing Contacts & Schedules

There are software applications that allow you to synchronize emails, calendar and contacts between your desktop and your mobile handheld. Some applications will allow you to share your calendar and contacts with colleagues or your assistant. This can be helpful, for example, when scheduling a group meeting by being able to view prospective participants' availability before scheduling a time.

Sharing Computer Files

File management and sharing can reduce redundant work across your organization. Documents can be organized for easy access by being stored in an organized hierarchy, by subject or by file type, on a shared network drive.

Security

There are several ways to mitigate the risks to sensitive or confidential information. You can create different shared network drives, and provide different employees access to different drives. You can protect your files from outsiders by installing firewall and file encryption software – both of which are included in the professional version of Microsoft Windows – on each employee's computer. Since most employees will at some point bring home work, you can have a company policy that requires firewall and file encryption software on all employees personal computers and requiring that they connect to the Internet through a secure connection (VPN). Use caution when synchronizing sensitive information with external servers or mobile devices as they have the potential to be easily compromised.

The copying of files by employees isn't usually as significant a risk as is an employee leaving with the knowledge they have gained, and that is only possible to protect that with reasonable non-disclosure and non-compete agreements. This is particularly true with something like software, where if a person has created software, an improved version can be created from scratch in a fraction of the time it took to create the original.

Electronic Communication

Legal Liability

Emails can potentially expose you to the same legal liability as if what you wrote were put in handwriting. While email is a less formal and verifiable medium than a hand written letter, it's still your thoughts put in writing.

Disclaimers

Investment banks, accounting and law firms have found it prudent to setup their email servers to automatically append a disclaimer to every outgoing email. A standard disclaimer usually states something to the effect of this is only the opinion of the sender, that it is not advice and may not represent the opinion of the company.

Reputational Risks

If you feel emotionally charged when writing a message, finish the message and let it sit overnight. Either leave the recipient's address blank or set it as your own email address. If you can't wait overnight, have at least one person read the email before you send it. You may find a better way to say what you want to get across.

Filtering

Most email software allows you to setup filtering rules for incoming messages such as moving all messages that are not from senders whose email address is in your address book to your junk mail folder. You can then periodically review your junk folder to see if any messages were put in there that you wanted.

Instant Messaging

Some organizations use internal instant messaging software as an alternative to internal phone calls or people getting up from their desks. For information on using instant messenger software to communicate with clients, see the chapter on Customer Service.

Videoconferencing

Videoconferencing can be done between any number of computers, and the meeting administrator can set which participant has the primary audio and video on the call at any given moment. There are a number of online video conferencing providers that can be found through an Internet search.

Websites

A web site is often the first place people turn to research your company.

Structure & Content

There is a basic structure that business websites tend to follow, typically including two primary sections: about the company, with sub sections including company history, executive bios, mission and vision statements, code of conduct, job openings, and contact information; and products and or services, with sub sections describing each offering along with ordering information.

Development

Sketch out a design for the template of your website and type up the content for each web page you want. Once this is done, you may want to bring in a web design professional. However, don't invest a lot of money in a web designer until you have a good sense of your desired structure, content and layout. They will help you to finalize these components, but it would be significantly more expensive and not necessarily more productive to have them work with you from the very beginning.

Interactive Websites

For websites that display information from a database, build the entire site using standard static web pages first, with sample data as placeholders. Once this is done, begin integrating your database. There are two reasons for this: it allows the design and the programming to be done by the appropriate individuals, and making changes to a web page after a database has been integrated takes exponentially more resources than getting the web pages done first and integrating the database second.

Domain Names

You can search for available domain names with a domain registrar, which can be found through an internet search. If you search for a domain name that has already been registered, you will usually be able to see the phone number and email address of the existing owner, who you can contact directly to see if they might be interested in selling. There are also a number of domain name auction sites that sell domain names that have already been registered.

Hosting

To put your website up on the Internet, the files for your website have to be put on a computer, running special software, that's always connected to the Internet. This service is provided by a large number of companies, and is known as web hosting. Web hosts can be found by searching for that term in a search engine.

Vision

Mission

&

Value

Statements

These statements are an opportunity to deliver a message to your employees, customers, investors and community — what do you want to say to them?

These statements can guide hiring, resource allocation and daily conduct. It may even make sense to post them near the entrance to your office so that employees see them every day when they come in.

These statements are only valuable to the extent that they are genuine and that leaders live by them. Some companies use them disingenuously to manage perceptions or to fill space on their website or in their annual report.

If you're starting a new company, you can create new vision, mission and value statements independently. If you're part of an existing company, leading the development of new statements in conjunction with employees will make them more comprehensive and increase employees' intellectual and emotional commitment to the statements.

Development

Start by looking at how you promote and pay people now, and determine what values they exhibit that you are rewarding. Identify what it takes to be successful in your company and record these values. It is most important to writing something that can and will be followed. Don't write something that won't be followed. If the values set by management aren't followed, the why follow the other decisions of management?

These values have to be lived from the top down and tied to compensation to be meaningful. If the values listed aren't values that you naturally demonstrate in your own leadership, the values statement will discredit your leadership.

Entrepreneurs

If you don't have any employees or clients yet, you're getting ahead of yourself here, and need to spend your time focusing on making sales.

www.ingramcontent.com/pod-product-compliance
Lightning Source LLC
Chambersburg PA
CBHW022037190326
41520CB00008B/623